WITHDRAWN
HARVARD LIBRARY
WITHDRAWN

Moral Concerns

By the Same Author (as Brenda Cohen)

Educational Thought: an introduction

Education and the Individual

Means and Ends in Education

Values: a symposium (ed. with Bryan Wilson)

Moral Concerns

Brenda Almond

(Reader in Philosophy and Education, University of Hull)

HUMANITIES PRESS INTERNATIONAL, INC.
Atlantic Highlands, NJ

First published in 1987 in the United States of America by
Humanities Press International, Inc., Atlantic Highlands, NJ 07716

© 1987 Humanities Press International, Inc.

Library of Congress Cataloging-in-Publication Data

Almond, Brenda.
  Moral concerns.

  1. Ethics.   2. Social ethics.   I. Title.
BJ1012.C64   1986   170   85–27202
ISBN 0–391–03372–7
ISBN 0-391-03422-7 (PBK)

All rights reserved. No reproduction, copy or transmission of this publication
may be made without written permission

MANUFACTURED IN THE UNITED STATES OF AMERICA

To the memory of my father,
Edward Almond

Contents

1. About Applied Philosophy   1
2. Environmental Values   13
3. Ethics, Sex and Law   27
4. The Limits of Toleration   43
5. Return to the Cave: New Directions for Philosophy of Education   57
6. Ethical Objectivity and Moral Education   69
7. Education and Contemporary Issues: The Problem of Political Relevance 77
8. Ethical Aspects of the Analytic Tradition   91
    G. E. Moore   91
    A. J. Ayer   101
9. An Ethical Paradox   113
10. Three Ethical Fallacies   125
11. Positive Values   135
    Index   151

Preface

The starting-point for ethical reflection is the question "What is to be done?" This is a wide rather than a narrow question, a political as well as a personal dilemma. Moral philosophy in its origins went hand in hand with theories of the state and discussions of law, citizenship, and politics. It is no more than a fulfilment of that ancient tradition that ethics should once again be seen as a practical enquiry. Moral concern in today's world is rightly perceived as a desire to find directions not only for personal life, but also for life in a social and legal setting. Indeed, it extends beyond that, to concern for political existence within the framework of an international order that provides conditions of peace, security, and personal self-determination, since these are, after all, essential prerequisites for the ethical life of the individual.

The essays gathered here do not pretend to cover the great range of issues that such an enterprise would demand. Nevertheless, they are offered as a partial contribution which aspires to be consistent with these ends. To some extent also, they cut across the bifurcation that has developed in academic ethics between the theoretical and the applied areas of the field. On the one hand, the essays here that deal with applied issues are the product of philosophical reflection and employ the traditional tools of philosophical analysis: criticism, counterexample, and a search for universalisable principles. On the other hand, the theoretical issues are approached from a practical point of view, even when it is the logic of moral language that is in question. Behind these theoretical discussions lies the question, what difference does this view—the resolution of this paradox, the way out of this dilemma—make to the way I may decide to act?

Given these concerns, then, it is appropriate that the first essay printed here deals with the notion of applied philosophy and attempts some reconciliation of the idea of philosophy as the most abstract of disciplines with the goal of "application"—a goal that suggests some direct relation to the world of facts. That tradition of moral philosophy that repudiates any relevance to the solution of substantive practical problems is rejected, but so, too, is, the notion of the moral "expert." It is argued, instead, that there is scope for a modest but nevertheless practical and constructive philosophical approach to a variety of issues of common concern.

The first such concern discussed here in chapter 2, is the environmental issue. Do we need, I ask, a new, non-human-centred ethic to determine our approach to environmental matters? And against some who have taken the view that a liberal and individualistic perspective on environmental issues is incompatible with concerted political action, I argue that such a position is, in fact, consistent with a search for broad international agreement on a morally informed approach to environmental issues.

In chapter 3, I turn from global to personal concerns and ask how far the state should, for social and economic reasons, impose through law the institutional structure of family relationships based on marriage as an exclusive sexual relationship. I ask, too, whether, on a more intimate level, it is possible to combine stability and flexibility in personal relationships.

Both these topics provide an illustration of the plurality of moral views and personal life-styles current in any one society and of the clash of interests and approaches revealed in the interactions of groups on the national and international scale. For some differences, tolerance is an appropriate response; for others it is not. In chapter 4, "The Limits of Toleration," I discuss where this line should be drawn. I argue that the limits of toleration are reached when the toleration principle itself comes into conflict with other deeply felt moral norms. Three cases in particular are taken as examples: (1) treatment of and attitudes to women under the Moslem religion; (2) the issue of the religious slaughter of animals; and (3) the issue of racism, including racism as signalled by membership in neo-Nazi organisations.

The question "What is to be done?" is not a question for simply our own generation, and so moral concern expresses itself most insistently in relation to education. In chapter 5, I consider the recent course of philosophy of education and argue for more direct concern about matters of substantive value in education. In chapter 6, "Ethical Objectivity and Moral Education" I address the more specific issue of moral education and ask whether its goal should be to secure conformity to society's conventions or to equip children to think for themselves morally, whatever conclusions they may come to. In chapter 7, I go on to raise the questions: To what extent should education be socially relevant? What part should politics play in the school curriculum? To what extent should schools and the education system be used or transformed to serve political and social ends?

Because my own thinking has been shaped within the analytic tradition, I include in chapter 8 two essays concerned with the development of the ethical aspects of the analytic tradition. These essays were originally presented as part of a course on analytic philosophy taught by academic

PREFACE   xi

"visitors" at unofficial seminars in Prague in 1982. The three remaining chapters discuss issues more narrowly defined as ethical. Chapter 9, "An Ethical Paradox," is included here, although previously published, both because of the interest it generated and because it is relevant to the issue of toleration and relativism. Chapter 10, "Three Ethical Fallacies" does a certain amount of essential ground clearing in relation to thinking about moral issues, and chapter 11, "Positive Values" presents the ethical position underlying the various "moral concerns" that form the common theme of this book.

Acknowledgments

I should like to thank the editor and publishers of the *Proceedings of the Aristotelian Society* for kindly giving me permission to reprint "Positive Values," and the editor and publishers of *Mind* for their permission to reprint "Three Ethical Fallacies" and "An Ethical Paradox." I also gratefully acknowledge the permission of the editor and publishers of the *Journal of Moral Education* to republish "Ethical Objectivity and Moral Education," and to the editor and publishers of *Educational Analysis*, vol. 4, no. 1 for permission to publish here "Return to the Cave: New Directions for Philosophy of Education." The above were published under the name Brenda Cohen.

I am grateful to the Philosophy Department of the Faculty of Arts at the Australian National University for providing me with excellent conditions for preparing this book for publication; to Thomas Mautner for reading and commenting on the final draft; and to Kanthi Fernando, Jean Ryan, and Reta Gear for their helpful efficiency in finalising the typescript.

1
About Applied Philosophy

> *Once [in 1942] when I had asked something about the study of ethics, Wittgenstein said it was strange that you could find books on ethics in which there was no mention of a genuine ethical or moral problem.*
> Report of conversation between Rush Rhees and Ludwig Wittgenstein[1]

This is, in a paradoxical way, an engaging admission. It is hard to explain, though, why no one else in philosophy should have found it strange. Note the date. In 1942 the world was being torn apart; convoys of mothers and children, teenagers and grandparents, the sick, the disabled, the brilliant, the talented were being conducted to human slaughterhouses for mechanised extermination. Scientists were engaged in a number of parallel races to produce horrific means of destruction in the form of chemical, biological, and ultimately atomic weapons. Random death, with accompanying destruction of the cultural artifacts of centuries, rained from the night skies onto sleeping cities. Secret decisions to resort to poison gas against invaders were being taken by respected statesmen. Torture of enemies, betrayal of friends; reprisals against the innocent; marital faithfulness put to extreme tests of separation, disfigurement, or disablement; deliberate and calculated expenditure of the lives of allies, friends, subordinates—all these ranked as moral problems of the first order in 1942.

And yet Wittgenstein and his interlocutor found difficulty in hitting upon a suitable "genuine" moral problem for discussion, and the one that they found most promising had nothing to do with any of these matters—it was as suitably timeless as most philosophical problems: a personal decision to be made between leaving a spouse and continuing to do useful work in cancer research.

Today, moral problems of an immediate and pressing practical nature are accorded more importance than this and the term *applied philosophy* has increasingly come into use as a description of a problem-directed approach. And yet the exact meaning of the term is far from having any clear definition.

Indeed, in contemporary philosophy, it could well be said that the term *applied philosophy* is acquiring a use without having been assigned any clear meaning. The *use* is widespread in Australia and in the United States, where it is particularly associated with the activities and investigations of philosophers in the fields of biomedical ethics, the prison service, hospitals, even public housing and other practical and professional areas. The idea of a philosophical, and more specifically, an ethical viewpoint being represented when decisions are made in the fields of medicine or legislation or any form of public policy-making is now widely accepted in the United States, where it is perfectly possible for philosophers to specialize in particular practical fields in which they are well-informed if not actually professionally qualified.

But if the answer that the meaning *is* the use seems too trite in this particular context, we are still left with the problem of trying to elucidate and justify the general term, as well as the flavour that it undoubtedly conveys, of philosophy intruding in practical fields. The problem about the term, as well as about the activity, is that it appears to bring together two notions that are more usually found in opposition: philosophy is the most abstract of enquiries, perhaps even best defined as the investigation of problems that cannot be solved by empirical enquiry, while *applied* suggests a direct relationship with the world of facts that is belied by this understanding of philosophy. In any case, there has been a whole tradition in philosophy this century, particularly in moral philosophy, of specifically repudiating any pretensions to the solution of practical problems. Ethics books published in English in this century have commonly started by directing their readers to their best friends, their parish priests, or their social worker for moral advice, and, in the best tradition of fair trading and accurate goods description, denying that what they have to say could be of any help to a reader with a genuine practical problem. The following quotations from works separated by a gap of almost fifty years, sum up this attitude well:

> We may say decisively that they [ethical judgements] do not belong to ethical philosophy. A strictly philosophical treatise on ethics should therefore make no ethical pronouncements.[2]

and

> This book is not about what people ought to do. It is about what they are doing when they *talk* about what they ought to do. Moral

philosophy, as I understand it, must not be confused with moralizing.³

But *philosophy* has already appeared in combinations that suggest practical application: *natural philosophy*, for example, for what is now physics, *social philosophy* for discussion of issues that have, on the whole, direct, practical political implications. But the first of these terms is now obsolete and the subjects represented by the other one have had low standing in the recent past. This latter fact may well be due to the success of logical positivism in particular in projecting the necessity of divorcing theoretical analysis from factual judgement and factual judgement from value. The original arguments for both separations are to be found in Hume and both can be seen as basic tenets of empiricism. As regards the first distinction Hume wrote:

> If we take in our hand any volume; of divinity, or school metaphysics, for instance; let us ask, Does it contain any abstract reasoning concerning quantity or number? No: Does it contain any experimental reasoning concerning matter of fact and existence? No. Commit it then to the flames. For it can contain nothing but sophistry and illusion.⁴

It is difficult to place moral reasoning about practical matters in either of these categories, and the tendency, since the logical positivists restated Hume's principle in the form of the verifiability principle (which limited meaningful assertion to [a] the empirical and [b] the analytic), has been for philosophers to restrict themselves to a form of philosophy that could be seen as the expansion of tautologies—in other words, analysis.

On the second point, which seems on the face of it even more damaging to the notion of reasoning to a practical (in the sense of moral) conclusion, Hume wrote:

> In every system of morality which I have hitherto met with, I have always remark'd that the author proceeds for some time in the ordinary way of reasoning, and establishes the being of a God, or makes observations concerning human affairs; when of a sudden I am surpris'd to find, that instead of the usual copulations of propositions, *is* and *is not*, I meet with no proposition that is not connected with an *ought*, or an *ought not*. This change is imperceptible; but is, however, of the last consequence. For as this *ought* or *ought not*, expresses some new relation or affirmation, 'tis necessary that it shou'd be observ'd and explain'd; and at the same time that a reason should be given, for what seems altogether inconceivable, how this new relation can be a

> deduction from others, which are entirely different from it. But as authors do not commonly use this precaution, I shall presume to recommend it to the readers; and am persuaded that this small attention wou'd subvert all the vulgar systems of morality, and let us see, that the distinction of vice and virtue is not founded merely on the relations of objects, nor is perceiv'd by reason.[5]

In the hands of the logical positivists, Hume's distinction, when combined with the verification principle, led to the emotivist theory of ethics. For the usefulness of ethical statements remained undeniable even though, in relation to the first distinction, it was clear they were not themselves statements of fact and, on the basis of the second distinction, that they could not be derived from facts. This could be explained by seeing them not as statements at all but as fulfilling some other function in the language (exhortation, the expression of emotion, and so on). So when the question was raised of how statements on one plane (the factual) could lead to, or be logically related to, pseudostatements on another plane (the emotive or evaluative), the answer seemed to be that they could not; and A. J. Ayer, for example, as the earlier quotation indicated, adopted this conclusion in *Language, Truth and Logic*. Critics of the theory noted that it had morally nihilistic consequences in practice, even if, in theory, moral nihilism was not implied. Nihilistic or not, however, it seemed to make moral judgements arbitrary, individual, even idiosyncratic. It invalidated the notion of moral argument. And it undermined any notion of a moral consensus. So, for these sorts of reasons, the fact-value distinction fell out of favour.

But the notion of applied philosophy seems to require one to look again at this distinction and to consider whether it is being unthinkingly disregarded in a way that will ultimately undermine the whole enterprise, or whether, or the contrary, it is an unnecessary limitation on enquiry. It must be conceded that the importance of the fact-value distinction can hardly be overestimated, and that this importance and influence could hardly flow from a wholly invalid distinction. The best-known arguments against it, those of Searle and Foot, have been subjected to exhaustive attack, and at least some of the ammunition directed at them must be judged as having found its target.[6] On the other hand, it would be unfortunate if it were to be thought that acceptance of the fact-value distinction, with whatever qualification may be necessary, means that thought must be marooned on one island or the other—the island of facts or the island of values—with no possibility of bridge building between the two. To admit this would be to admit that philosophy can have nothing to say about the pressing dilemmas of life in the twentieth century. Briefly, it can be said that *values* must be informed by the *facts* of human psychology, sociology, biology, and history if they are to stand any chance of gaining the widespread support and endorsement that is necessary for values to play any important role in human affairs. But this is not to say that they must be, in a logical sense, a derivation from these facts. Nor is it to suggest that values that have this capacity for widespread endorsement will necessarily be accepted by everybody, or even by the majority. To work for their acceptance is a political enterprise that will be engaged in by those who believe that they have discovered the "right answers." So, in one sense, there are, objectively, right answers in ethics, that is, from the "internal" viewpoint of anyone making a moral judgement; but in another sense, it is true that, as the subjectivists state, moral truth is a matter of opinion. But this is a judgement from outside—from a position that it is not open to any of us as participants in the world of moral practice and decision to make. This is to say that it is a logical error actually to endorse, as subjectivists try to do, the idea of the validity of each person's individual, isolated moral judgement, for built into the notion of moral value is the notion of generality if not universality. In other words, we necessarily judge for others as well as for ourselves when we make a moral judgement. But in forming such judgements, we need not arrive at the point of appraisal like newborn, nonsocial entities and will do well to draw on the wealth of human experience to take our judgements out of the sphere of individual eccentricity and arbitrariness and into the realm of rational acceptability.

At the root of this sort of approach lies the view that it is possible to see a relationship between facts and values, theory and practice, between what is and what ought to be, that does not flout the demands of logic, clarity, or sound reasoning. In particular, it is to say that there is nothing incoherent in regarding moral responses as responses to the *facts* of situations, and the way in which we deal with the situations as a result of those responses as yet more facts.

It is the second sort of facts that feature specifically in the standard range of interests covered by the term *applied philosophy*; for example, when it investigates such questions as what strategy to adopt when confronted with the fact of a severely handicapped newborn baby or the social facts of unwanted pregnancies; what policy to adopt given the factual possibilities of nuclear weaponry or the practical consequences of a purely short-term approach to profit where production of crops is maintained by the use of chemicals and pesticides. A willingness to become engaged with such problems is clearly part of the positive content of applied philosophy. But for further illumination of the concept it would be better to proceed negatively rather than positively and to say something about what the term does *not* involve rather that what it does.

To begin with, it need not involve any claim that philosophers have a monopoly on human wisdom or morality, although this is what a contributor to the *Salisbury Review* appears to believe. Pointing out that Bradley saw ethics as aimed at truth rather than practice, and relating his comments to the foundation of the Society for Applied Philosophy[7], David Bell wrote:

> We have become used to the idea that morality is not a science; the "emotivist" view of ethics has taught us that. We have also become used to something sometimes called "first order ethics," a licence for the advocacy by intellectuals of a variety of "first order" moral views in the pages of academic journals and elsewhere. Not hunting or consuming animals, giving ladies their due, weighing the justifications of abortion, pondering the possibility of a just war fought with nuclear weapons, all these issues and many more have recently been the subject of this enquiry. Bradley would have had, I dare say, no great objection to such concerns. But he would have objected to dignifying them by the title of "moral philosophy." He would have observed, for example, that the recent founders of the Society for Applied Philosophy are not conspicuously more endowed with practical wisdom or the requisite experience and knowledge than many others of the population who might (on what ground?) be excluded from that body. He might have gone on to observe that, built into the very foundations of such a body, is that particular form of rationalism which we know as casuistry.
> ... The common-room enthusiasts for animal rights may harbour the curious belief that discursive reason is a potent instrument for altering the common moral consciousness. But Bradley would deny that they have any right to name the fruits of their labours "moral philosophy."[8]

Before considering the overall view expressed here, one or two specific aspects of this criticism deserve comment. The writer lists some typical concerns of what he calls "first order" ethics—animals, women, and nuclear war—and he suggests that discussion of these issues would be "dignified" if they were conceded to be moral philosophy. This is to imply that as things are, these discussions rank at some lower level. It is interesting to reflect on a scale of philosophical values that rates discussion of issues involving humanity, kindness, justice, and human survival lower than abstract discussion, which is defined, apparently, only by the fact that it avoids such issues.

Then there is the charge of *casuistry* (although it is some consolation to see that this vice is attributed, too, to Mill and Sidgwick). Two meanings are given in the Oxford English Dictionary for the term. A casuist may be a person, especially a theologian, who resolves cases of conscience, duty, and so on, or the casuist may be a sophist, a quibbler. I believe we are to understand the first of these meanings here, although clearly the more usual association today would be with the second and less-flattering interpretation. The charge, then, seems to be that applied philosophy or "first order ethics" attempts to determine what actually is our duty in a particular case. It is true that Bradley did seek to limit the scope of ethics, saying, for example, "Ethics has not to make the world moral, but to reduce to theory the morality current in the world." Nevertheless, he also wrote a famous chapter with the title "My Station and its Duties," thus showing that he had, despite these austere remarks, some concern himself, as a philosopher, with the resolution of duty. But the attack here becomes an attack on moral system building, and in particular on utilitarianism. The suggestion is that systems must come into conflict with "the untutored moral consciousness." This may be so, but it is wrong to see a weighting in favour of systems or of utilitarianism in the "very foundations" of a society for applied philosophy. On the contrary, the search for common values that is mentioned in the rubric of the particular society that is the subject of Bell's attack could well proceed from the deliverances of an "untutored moral consciousness"—from intuitionism rather than utilitarianism.[9]

On the general direction of these criticisms, however, one thing at least must be conceded. This is that it would be an unjustifiable *hubris* on the part of contemporary moral philosophers to claim that any of their number could be regarded as moral experts and asked to pronounce definitively on the ethical and philosophical aspects of, for example, world poverty, energy policy, or human relationships on behalf of everybody else. It would appear that there may be some people without this reluctance, and, as a result, ugly terms like *biomedical ethicist* are gaining currency. But the term *ethicist* is as objectionable as the blurring of notions that it covers; not, this time, the blurring of the line between values and facts, but the blurring of the line between being a moral philosopher and being an authority on what is right and wrong. The possibility of being the second would seem to rule out the point of being the first, and it would be a valuable self-denying ordinance to insist that applied philosophy must remain first and foremost philosophy. What the term suggests, in fact, is a willingness to reflect on and reason about what is right or wrong in the difficult and controversial areas in question. Where, as a result of this process, someone has arrived at a personal conviction or conclusion on an issue, then we might expect that person to use the tools of philosophy—clarification and analysis—to make out the best possible case for that position or point of view. It is only in this last respect that they may be allowed to claim a degree of authority or superiority. Philosophers may well be expected to be more at home than most people in the pursuit of argument and analysis. But if they are, this is simply because they are privileged to have had more practice than most people, and not because they have benefited from some esoteric initiation. To say this is to look back to an older conception of philosophy—one that carried with it an older conception of the philosopher as an honest and open seeker after truth, a participant in an early Socratic dialogue, rather than a Platonic exponent of the good and the true.

It means that the philosopher in applied fields should welcome the participation of experts or professionals in the field in question, possibly aspiring to fruitful collaboration, but in any case seeing expertise and reflective argument as a potent and fruitful combination.

However, another negative proviso is necessary here. To repudiate the notion of philosophers as moral authorities is not to embrace another prevalent conception: that an issue or problem can be resolved or dissolved by a dispassionate philosophical study that approaches alternative viewpoints with the same degree of detachment. It may be that a degree of commitment to a point of view is more likely to throw light on a practical problem or cultural question than is a posture of uninvolved neutrality. *Merely* to clarify is to make very little progress and may amount to no more than simply laying out rival arguments side by side, like cold fish on a slab.

But, of course, on some issues it may be impossible, or at least very difficult, to reach a conclusion. On these issues—which might include, for example, abortion or euthanasia—ultimate perplexity or simply the agony of indecision is an understandable human response. But practice, unlike theory, compels to decision. Having weighed the pros and cons of Cruise missile deployment or capital punishment, it is necessary to deploy or not to deploy, to execute or to imprison. So even on these extremely difficult issues, philosophical defence of a position may be more helpful than the traditional balancing act of recent academic writing. But on other issues—on torture, for instance, on terror bombing, or on freedom of thought—such academic posturing may be positively offensive and counterproductive.

But this is not to attempt to justify arbitrary prejudice. Underlying the selection of that particular list of potential topics of discussion and the assumption of a common moral viewpoint upon them is a belief in a certain distinctive range of values. The notion of applied philosophy might, therefore, profitably be extended to include the identification, justification, and discussion of values capable of commanding widespread acceptance and endorsement in the contemporary world. But there might well be an interim stage in which values that are deeply and instinctively felt by those who have reflected upon them, and that have this kind of potential, nevertheless cannot in the short term command any such universal allegiance. In this case, the onus will be on those who have arrived at a deep and considered conviction to become, through argument and persuasion, proselytizers for their point of view.

If this is a political rather than a purely philosophical task, then to this extent it involves acceptance of the thesis that the notion of applying philosophy has political as well as moral overtones. But there is nothing odd or unfamiliar about this. For philosophy has frequently appeared as a power in the world, particularly when it has taken on the ideological or theoretic forms of Marxism, Catholicism, or Islam. There is no reason to suppose that other types of philosophy, including even a critical liberal philosophy that starts from empiricist assumptions, may not be influential, too, when their implicit value basis becomes explicit. In Eastern Europe, for instance in Czechoslovakia, there are people who are prepared to engage in the study of this type of philosophy even at the risk of personal security and prosperity. And in South America, too, there are examples of philosophy providing a focus for the continuation of the tradition of open and disinterested enquiry that military regimes attempt to suppress. So philosophy itself, even in its modest and unassuming Socratic posture, can be a political or social force. And this, it seems to me, is the ultimate interpretation of *applied philosophy*—philosophy as itself an agent of change.

The more common understanding of *applied philosophy* must, though, continue to be the primary one. Essentially, this is the notion of philosophy applied to pressing contemporary issues and problems in a whole range of areas. These include a broad group of problems in the applications of science and technology (e.g., ecological and environmental issues, and biomedical questions such as *in vitro* fertilisation, abortion, and euthanasia), problems of law and society (e.g., family relationships;

political protest and dissent; individual rights and the limits of government), and issues in a number of other specific areas such as education, business, and medicine.

In relation to all such issues there are essentially two different kinds of contribution that can be made by philosophy. One is to fulfil its uncontroversial function of clarification through criticism, analysis, and the use of argument. Although this function is uncontroversial, philosophers should be aware of a public relations problem here, since in a number of practical fields where philosophers have intervened with this primary objective, there has been a resistance on the part of professionals in the field who are, understandably, unable to hold their hand indefinitely from the plough while a perfect conceptual analysis of farming is sought. So the analytic contribution to education, for example, has unfortunately had, for the most part, a deadening effect on the philosophy of education. But, inevitably, applied philosophy will be more closely identified with the second type of contribution. This is direct consideration of substantive ethical positions in relation to those aspects of contemporary life listed above. The kind of "solution" offered, though, is likely to be in terms of the *principles* that should guide decision making—legal, economic, political, social, personal—in relation to any particular problem, rather than a blueprint for action.

This objective cannot in the end be carried out without some investigation of the values in terms of which any ethical appraisal is bound to be conducted. The requirement for these values is, as has already been suggested, that they should have, at least potentially, widespread appeal— some capacity for being held as common human values. It follows from this—although it must be recognised that this is a contentious claim—that they must be derived neither from religion nor from any existing political grouping, since either of these sources is ultimately divisive. The difficulty of justifying values that are not founded on authority ensures a place for theoretical ethics within the framework of applied philosophy as well as for the more recognisably "applied" task of drawing ethical conclusions where possible and appropriate.

It is possible, then, to have a reasonably clear picture of the enterprise, whatever detractors may say. Some people might still feel, though, that a reason needs to be given for going in this direction. I can best offer this in terms of a personal reflection that relates to the points made at the beginning of this essay. I once had occasion to refer to an article on Kant published in the 1940s that concerned a possible link between Kant's Categorical Imperative and the German ideal of unconditional obedience to authority as it had been manifested in the Second World War. And it occurred to me then for the first time how very odd it was that perusal of philosophical journals that had been published throughout the war years—through, in other words, years that included the horrors of obliteration bombing, racial persecution and genocide, and the dropping of atomic bombs on civilian populations—should reveal little or nothing of this backdrop to philosophical reflection, apart from isolated oblique references of this sort. Marx, in the nineteenth century, had not been indifferent to the horrors and abuses prevalent in his time, and yet it seemed as though a liberal philosophy of a later date, which considered itself to have benefited from twentieth-century enlightenment, *could* display this indifference. Of course, this is not the whole picture, for certain very important books in the liberal tradition published just after the war *were* inspired by reflection on what had passed—books such as Popper's *The Open Society and its Enemies*, Hayek's *The Road to Serfdom*, and Talmon's *The Origins of Totalitarian Democracy*. But the observation about the journals remains striking. It seemed to me then worth asking whether there might not be similarly glaring features of our time that are so large a part of the landscape that it does not occur to us to do other than ignore them, but that will strike our successors as the things that *should* have concerned us most.

I think there is no doubt that there are, and that if we *have* successors, then one of these striking features of our moral landscape is the threat of self-extermination posed by the buildup of nuclear weapons and by the policy of deterrence. But this is merely a shadow and a threat, and the dominating actuality of our time is probably not this but the widespread use of torture and extermination as political and judicial weapons, together with the tendency of human beings to create hierarchical structures of power, that makes these abuses possible.

At the same time, the most valuable *moral* notion for our time is probably that of human rights, since this is a moral concept that has already shown itself, whatever the abuses of the notion, to have the power to transcend boundaries of culture and nation—to be widely understood and capable of providing a focus for action.

Of course, none of this is to suggest that all other philosophical activity and investigation should cease in the light of the overwhelming priority these issues carry with them. On the contrary, the philosophical traditions of two thousand years of inquiry are part of what it is important to maintain by the elimination of both the threat and the realities just listed—the threat because if it were realised it would destroy civilisation and culture along with humanity; the realities because they make impossible all cultural and intellectual pursuits for those physically caught up in them. My argument is simply that it is important that *some* philosophers who see themselves as part of that long tradition should seek to find ways in which their discipline can contribute directly to the solution of these problems.

Notes

Some of the views expressed here were put forward by Brenda Cohen and Anthony O'Hear, in the editorial in the first issue of the *Journal of Applied Philosophy*.

1. Rush Rhees, "Some Developments in Wittgenstein's View of Ethics," *Philosophical Review* 74 (1965): 21.
2. A. J. Ayer, *Language, Truth and Logic* (London: Gollancz, 1936), 103.
3. W. D. Hudson, *Modern Moral Philosophy* (London: Macmillan, 1970), p. 1.
4. D. Hume, *An Enquiry Concerning Human Understanding*, ed. P. H. Nidditch, sect. 13, pt. 3 (London: Oxford University Press, 1977), p. 165.
5. D. Hume, *A Treatise of Human Nature*, ed. P. H. Nidditch, bk. 3, sect. 1, (London: Oxford University Press, 1978), pp. 469–70.
6. See also discussion in chap. 5.
7. The Society for Applied Philosophy referred to here was founded in 1982 by Brenda Cohen and Anthony O'Hear. Its first presidents have been A. J. Ayer and (from 1985 to this writing) R. M. Hare.
8. David R. Bell, "F . H. Bradley as a Conservative Thinker," *Salisbury Review*, Autumn 1983.
9. The rubric of the Society includes the following statement of aims:

> The Society for Applied Philosophy is established to provide a focus for philosophical research with a direct bearing on areas of practical concern which are capable of being illuminated by the critical, analytic approach characteristic of philosophy and by direct consideration of questions of value. . . . It is . . . committed to the notion of human values capable of transcending narrow or local interests and so appealing to individuals across the boundaries of nations, classes and cultures. It sees the identification, justification and discussion of these values as part of its task.

2
Environmental Values

Three images provide a focus for thought.

- A child plays on a beautiful beach in Cumbria. The sun shines. The sea gleams, the child adorns a lovingly constructed sand castle with some seaweed washed up by the waves.
- A woman tends her country garden somewhere in England. The cottage borders on fertile farmland. The summer peace and tranquillity are broken only by the sound of a low-flying small plane passing overhead.
- An Italian family sit down for their evening meal in a home that is the fruit of the labour of the parents. There is a possibility that another child has been conceived and the parents are pleased with the prospect.

But in each case the tranquillity is temporary, the happiness illusory. For an unseen—indeed an unseeable—menace overlies the scene. A year later, the parents of the child in Cumbria live in fear that pollution of the shoreline, caused by radioactive emissions into the sea from nearby Windscale (now Sellafield), may make their child a youthful leukaemia victim. The woman gardener is paralysed and wheelchair bound, endeavouring to recover damages for the air-borne poisoning she received in the aerial spraying of crops routinely practiced by her farming neighbour. And the family in Seveso in Italy is excluded indefinitely from their home, which is heavily contaminated with dioxin and are, moreover, the parents of a five-month-old child handicapped by gross deformities.

It is the generalisation of these particular cases that has provided fuel for the fire of the environmentalist movement, and in its philosophical manifestation has raised the question of whether there may not be obligations on the part of humans to respect the natural world. This may be expressed as a demand for a new ecological ethic expressed in terms of values inherent in nature itself—environmental values. Such a transformation of emphasis has sometimes been referred to as a paradigm shift in ethical thought. Up to now, ethics, whether secularly or religiously based, has been human-centred. Aldo Leopold, in his seminal work *A Sand County Almanac*, traced three stages of ethical thought: an early stage in which ethics is seen as governing relations between individuals, a later stage in which it is seen as governing relations between individual and society, and a necessary third stage of which he says: "The extension of ethics to this third element in human environment is . . . an evolutionary possibility and an ecological necessity." Of this third type of ethic he writes: "An ethic, ecologically, is a limitation on freedom of action in the struggle for existence," and, in a much quoted definition: "A thing is right when it tends to preserve the integrity, stability and beauty of the biotic community. It is wrong when it tends otherwise."[1]

In the environmental debate, certain key words recur. Words whose connotation is favourable are *conservation, preservation, wilderness*. Words with an unfavourable connotation are *pollution, waste, exploitation*, and *depletion of resources*. On the one side is set the notion of sympathy or one-ness with nature, whether for practical utilitarian or spiritual, quasi-mystical reasons. On the other is set the notion of human *hubris*—a Greek notion for which, significantly, no English word has been coined, but which carries essentially the idea of man claiming the authority and privileges of the gods. In line with this, we have the notion of man as dominator, man the species-ist, vandalising his physical setting and making it unfit for himself as well as for other species that he unthinkingly and for short-term gain ousts. As the authors of *Only One Earth*, an unofficial report commissioned for the United Nations Conference on the Human Environment wrote: "There is no doubt indeed that most of our present environmental difficulties originate from man's ecological misbehaviour. Increasingly we consider ourselves not as lodgers on the earth, but as its landlords; we identify progress with the conquest of the external world even if this means destruction of those parts of nature which we assume—often erroneously—to be irrelevant to our welfare."[2] So where does value lie? And where does the balance of good and evil fall? With those who advance man's prosperity by "making the desert bloom like a rose" or with those peoples, like the former nomadic inhabitants of Israel, like the Australian Aborigines or the North American Indians, who have lived on the surface of the planet Earth but left their passage and stay unrecorded in the ecology and topography of their land? In answering this question there may be a clash between intuitive and more considered responses. *Beauty*, *nature*, and *endangered species* are evocative words, and there may well be an initial presumption in their favour when they are counterposed against man's domination by his own machines, the concrete wastelands at the heart of many modern cities, factory-farming, and pollution of the atmosphere and ocean, that carry with them the threat, perhaps, of the death of the planet and the end of human existence. But not everyone makes this value judgement or accepts this assessment. We may set on one side vitriolic and blinkered critics like the American writer Ayn Rand, who, writing of "ecological crusaders—who would pollute any stream by stepping into it," says:

> When man's greatest benefactor, technology, is denounced as an enemy of mankind . . . when the great emancipator, the automobile, is attacked as a public menace, and highways are decried as a violation of the wilderness—when bleary-eyed, limp-limbed young hobos of both sexes chant about the evil of labor-saving devices, and demand that human life be devoted to the grubby hand-planting of truck-gardens, and to garbage disposal—when alleged scientists stretch, fake or suppress scientific evidence in order to panic the ignorant about the interplanetary perils augured by some such omen as the presence of mercury in tuna fish . . . it is time to grasp that we are not dealing with man-lovers, but with killers.[3]

But we must take more seriously philosophical critics of the ecological movement and those who present a considered challenge to the evidence of a planetary threat on which that movement is based. These include those who believe, like H. J. McCloskey, that the "ecological crisis" will be solved by science and technology themselves and that it is to science and technology that we must turn for solutions to the problems they have brought about: problems, for example, of depletion of resources, environmental damage, pollution, over-population, harmful pesticides and chemicals, extermination of species, and nuclear risks of peace and war. Solutions are problematic, but the facts themselves, or at least present and past facts, are not substantially in dispute and it would be as well to indicate briefly what some of these facts are.

The initial alarm, as far as the general public was concerned, was sounded with the publication in 1962 of Rachel Carson's *Silent Spring*, but subsequently many international agencies and groupings have identified and discussed a whole range of problems precipitated by man's increasing mastery of technology and exploitation of his knowledge without consideration of global and long-term consequences.[4] The 1972 Stockholm Conference on the Human Environment organised by the United Nations was pr_ pt_ by a sense of urgency concerning world poverty, population incr ase, depletion of resources, and pollution. It recognised the problem of the disparity between developed and developing countries that makes the latter understandably averse to any suggestion—even if the affluent nations themselves would find it acceptable—of deindustrialisation or a retreat from the pursuit of material prosperity. This implies acceptance of energy-producing processes that, as things stand, must inevitably bring in their train some environmental pollution, with the generation of nuclear energy by nuclear means presenting the most intractable problems.

Among the undisputed present consequences of industrialised processes are the pollution of rivers, lakes, and oceans by a constant flow of toxic substances, with the Mediterranean providing an example of what happens when the upper limit of what even a massive water region can absorb is reached. (Sixteen countries have now combined in an Action Plan designed to control the emission of untreated sewage, detergents, pesticides, heavy metals, industrial chemicals and oil that have been the cause of the Mediterranean's problems.)

Other recognised current problems include various forms of air pollution, both those such as smog, caused by automobile emissions in cities, that affect people immediately, and, more controversially, those such as chlorofluorocarbons (CFCs) that threaten the ozone layer protecting the atmosphere of the earth. There is also the problem of acid rain that, in addition to its effects on forests in Continental Europe, has produced dying lakes in Scandinavia and the prospect in Canada that many of its lakes could become fishless over the next decade.

The use of chemicals and pesticides in agriculture and animal husbandry constitutes a third area for concern, for while their use has immeasurably increased productivity and the supply of food, it has made the ingestion of these chemicals virtually unavoidable in a normal diet. Any catalogue of environmental hazards currently occupying the world's scientific and economic experts must include, too, agricultural problems of desertification and erosion of soil, leading to large-scale famine and accentuating the North-South divide. This divide itself is a reminder that other indisputable contemporary facts with environmental implications are the growth of human population and the uneven distribution of economic resources.

But it is the future consequences of these present facts that provoke most controversy. The findings of the Club of Rome as published in *The Limits of Growth* were that time is running out for humanity to face up to and deal with its problems.[5] Its authors recount an appropriate French riddle: there is a pond on which a water lily grows. The plant doubles its size each day and would cover the pond entirely in thirty days if left unchecked. If you decide to wait until the plant covers half the pond, which day will you have to deal with it? The answer is that this will be the twenty-ninth day. It is the argument of the Club of Rome that humankind has now reached the twenty-ninth day in respect of most of the environmental threats just listed. Its findings have been challenged by some, decried as alarmist by others, but, in fact, the growth of officially sponsored environment-monitoring agencies in the past decade under the United Nations Environment Programme (UNEP) suggest that at the least an attitude of caution is rationally justified.

It is, of course, the question of value that concerns us here rather than straightforward questions of expediency. We may, in other words, endorse Leopold's claim that ethics and aesthetics, as well as economics, should determine the use we make of the earth. Nevertheless, it would be a mistake to set questions of rational expediency in opposition to questions of value too readily. As H. H. Iltis has written: "Not until man accepts his dependency on nature and puts himself in place as part of it, not until then does man put men first. This is the greatest paradox of human ecology."[6]

The fate of humanity is bound up, then, with a harmonious solution to humanity's technical planetary problems. Searching for technical solutions alone, though, may not be the best method of approach, and for at least some of these problems, technical solutions may be unachievable. As the authors of *The Limits of Growth* point out, this must be so in the case of the arms race, racial tensions, and unemployment.

On the wider range of environmental issues, they write: "Applying technology to the natural pressures that the environment exerts against any growth process has been so successful in the past that a whole culture has evolved around the principle of fighting against limits rather than learning to live within them. This culture has been reinforced by the apparent immensity of the earth and its resources and by the relative smallness of man and his activities."[7]

Hirsch has added to this assessment the argument that the limits to growth may be social as well as physical and that the pursuit of economic growth, may, paradoxically, result in individuals satisfying less, rather than more, of their aspirations.[8]

The case for adjusting to a reversed assessment, in which the finitude of the earth and its resources is recognised and there is an acceptance of the natural limits to growth, may be argued for, then, on both scientific and economic grounds. And in place of purely technical solutions, both expert opinion and common sense suggest a need for a transformation of perspective. Such a changed perspective will involve a new order of values more appropriate to the new order of problems that have been created by the speed at which man's scientific knowledge and technical expertise has overtaken his reflective and moral capacities. Indeed, the situation is one that lends particular point and pertinency to the Genesis story of Adam and Eve, the first parents of the human race. The tree of knowledge in the creation story was the tree of knowledge of good and evil—and the story foreshadowed mankind's need for a moral sense to provide a check to the indiscriminate directions in which the pursuit of knowledge might lead.

But can there be an ecological ethic? Such distinguished contributors to the debate as Passmore[9] have argued that there cannot be, and that the moral categories we already employ, those based on attributing value only to human experience and human consciousness, are sufficient to generate all the obligations that may be binding on us as far as nature is concerned. McCloskey has argued more strongly still that so-called ecological values are actually in conflict with important values implicit within liberal and humanistic ethical traditions, in particular those of individual freedom and autonomy, justice and respect for human rights. McCloskey argues against the notion that nature is ethically good, pointing out that it can frequently be harsh, savage, and cruel. His view is that environmental concern is a luxury of the wealthy nations at the expense of the poor. Politically, he believes that ecological concern is elitist and dictatorial, and that morally it is based on a narrow and unattractive puritanical asceticism.[10]

These political and social implications must be explored later, but first it must be conceded that there is a shift in thinking needed if human beings are to move from a purely human-centred system of morals. Indeed, the first shift needed may be one of language rather than of thought, for a language of values may meet environmentalist needs better than a language of narrowly defined morality and, specifically, of duties. This is not to say that it is impossible to formulate an ethical position that attaches a value to inanimate nature in terms of a traditional terminology of duties. In "Duties concerning Islands," for example, Mary Midgley lists nineteen categories of beings, outside the category of other equal human beings, to whom we might consider duties were owed. These include the dead, posterity, the insane, animals, plants, works of art, oneself, and God. This suggests that it does make sense to consider duties not simply as relationships between conscious and thinking equals. It thus makes it possible to claim that Defoe's Robinson Crusoe might have had some kind of duty to his island—a small-scale version of man's duty to the planet Earth—that would have been violated had he considered wantonly destroying his island on departure.[11]

Nevertheless, the question at issue is probably better posed in the language of values rather than the language of duties. It can then be presented as the question of whether nature, animate and inanimate, has value in itself—intrinsic value. Does a lake or a mountain have value? Or, in the words of another contributor to this debate, concerned to add a legal to the moral dimension, should trees have standing?[12] The question is essentially whether the attribution of value is necessarily and essentially a response of a human being to what is external to him or her, or whether value is in the world—something that human beings discover, recognise, may become aware of, or may ignore and fail to appreciate.

The answer to this may be a mixture of truism and novelty comparable to the truistic/novel claim that objects depend on us for their perceived existence—that *esse* is *percipi*. The argument originally advanced by Bishop Berkeley in the eighteenth century may be construed as the claim that there is no way we can conceive of an object of vision that is not seen or a sound that is unheard, since our imagining has the function of introducing a perceiver into the structure of the thought experiment.[13] In a precisely parallel way, we may argue that we cannot formulate the notion of objects of value outside the experience of human beings—though we can well imagine that there can be such objects to which we do not in fact have physical access—since in imagining them we introduce ourselves as valuers into the imagined situation. So we may attempt to compare the value of two worlds at the outer reaches of the universe, both equally beautiful but one devoid of living creatures capable of sentient awareness. Can this second world, we may ask, have value? If it vanished in some cosmic cataclysm, would this matter? It seems clear that in formulating the hypothesis we have removed our imagined worlds, both the first and the second, from the realm of what is truly inaccessible to human valuing. In other words, we do not need an objective sense of value to attach value to inanimate nature, mainly because the contrast in this case between subjective and objective value is unreal. This is not the subjectivist claim that values are in ourselves only—our creation—any more than Berkeley's argument really entailed that the external world was the creation of our perceptual faculties. It is rather the claim that it is through the medium of our moral sense that we must make judgements as to what has worthwhile existence, what counts and what does not.

In this, we are quite capable of placing our own role as observers on the scale of significance it merits. This may well be much lower than a standard human-centred morality or ethics suggests. The philosopher M. R. Cohen wrote of "the unique privilege of being for a brief space a spectator of the great drama of existence in which solar systems are born and destroyed—a drama in which our part as actors is of infinitesimal significance."[14]

Our problem, however, is that we are no longer mere bystanders and inconspicuous observers on the shores of the universe, but have acquired the capacity to destroy at least our own world. And philosophies such as utilitarianism, at least in its more plausible forms, are incapable of providing an argument against destruction because where there are no sentient beings there can be no suffering. Other elements beyond the scope of standard utilitarianism that it may be necessary to take account of in a full environmental ethic are suggested by R. Goodin in a reflective article; in particular he argues that special weight ought to be given to irreversibility in our environmental decision making and that we should beware of opting for gains that are necessarily short-lived.[15] These voluntary limitations and this changed perception of our own species' place in the universe may be summed up under the general heading of humility as the first value in a new environmental ethic.

But a more fundamental ethical perspective is that of holism, which supplies a second element for an ecological ethic, the idea of harmony as an environmental value. Children are sometimes given a set of Russian dolls as playthings. These are a set of wooden dolls of graduated sizes that fit neatly into each other. The perspectives of the telescope and the microscope show us that we are somewhere in the middle of just such a set of Russian dolls. Just as the parts and cells of our bodies form organic unities of matter that is constantly being replenished by death and regeneration, so, there is cause to believe, our universe itself is such a system. Between these extremes of the galactic and the microscopic, the world in which we live can be regarded as a living and self-renewing whole, and humanity itself is, in W. H. Harding's words "a set within a hierarchical system of sets."[16]

One consequence of accepting this, though, is that our judgements of value may not conform to our most immediate taste and interest. As J. B. Callicot has observed,

> The natural world as actually constituted is one in which one being lives at the expense of others. . . . There are desire, pleasure in the satisfaction of desire, acute agony attending injury, frustration and

chronic dread of death. But these experiences are the psychological substance of living. To live *is* to be anxious about life, to feel pain and pleasure in a fitting mixture, and sooner or later to die. That is the way the system works. If nature as a whole is good, then pain and death are also good.[17]

Callicot adds that the aspiration for pleasure without pain is "biologically preposterous." This is consistent with the Routleys' definition of environmental value as "Diversity of systems and creatures, naturalness, integrity of systems, stability of systems, harmony of systems."[18]

Callicot's observation is made in order to point to a potential gulf between those environmentalists concerned to focus on the rights of nonhuman animals and those, like Leopold, for whom a concern for the environment is not inconsistent with the hunting, killing, and eating of animals, though for both groups, modern methods of rearing animals for food—the creation of 'animal machines'—will be objectionable. This potential gulf is widened by the claim by some environmentalists that the enforcement of animal rights in an unqualified way would result in some animal species reaching plague proportions, thus damaging the ecosystem in another but equally unacceptable way. But it would be absurd to construe defence of animal rights as a demand for humans to intervene in the role of police to enforce the preservation of individual animal lives against their natural predators. Nevertheless, it is arguable that vegetarianism, with the change of land use to the raising of crops that this would involve, is yet another way in which man might interfere with the natural balance of the environment. Here we may distinguish between the morally respect-worthy gesture of an individual in personally deciding not to live by the death of other living creatures and the universalised demand for a total change in human dietary habits—particularly if this demand includes the repudiation of fish, consumption of which, overfishing apart, involves no assault at all on the ecology of the earth or the habitats of other nonhuman creatures. (These observations leave ample space for an animal rights movement concerned with methods of raising animals for food, conditions of slaughter, the preservation of species, and the issue of vivisection.)

The holistic approach to the ecological issue, then, is consistent with varying practical responses. The key ethical concept it involves is, however, clear. It is that of harmony: of creature with creature, of creature with habitat. Harmony carried to its extreme manifestation is identity, so it is understandable that such a view could, in the end, become a modern form of mysticism or pantheism. The notion of everything that exists composing an organic whole takes us back in the end to the earliest approaches to Western philosophy—the Greek understanding that nothing comes out of nothing; that nothing ever really ceases to exist, but that existence constitutes an endless cycle of transformations of material. And just as that notion led to the Stoic ethic of acceptance and adaptation—to a recognition of necessity and to a choice of intellectual rather than purely material values—so a parallel awareness in our own and our successors' generations, this time based on more accurate scientific and ecological understanding, could produce a similar reorientation of values and a general rejection of utilitarian and materialistic values that would bring Western thought closer to the religious and philosophical attitudes of the East and of some primitive peoples.

This phenomenon of progressive and developing awareness is, of course, what is distinctive in the human animal. The insights and discoveries of individuals do not die with them but become part of the collective consciousness. It was this notion of objective knowledge that Popper saw as providing the basis for a new approach to epistemology. He used the term *World Three* to describe an entity that is the product of individual human thinkers, but that cannot be equated with either the subjective world of individual mental experience or the external world of material objects. He saw the human ability to leave behind through culture and pass on through education individual insights, knowledge, and conjectures as the condition and ground of scientific progress.[19] That this collective consciousness should also develop a collective conscience—a universal concept of value—would not be an absurd demand, nor would it be an inappropriate goal for human beings to set themselves. Otherwise, to follow a metaphor devised by the atomic physicist Heisenberg, mankind's position may be compared to that of people travelling in a boat with so much steel in its composition that its compass has ceased to work effectively.[20]

But in practical terms, the application of such common human values to ecological problems could only be achieved through international political agencies capable of monitoring global hazards on a global scale. Here the charges of those who see this as a demand for an "ecological dictatorship" necessarily in conflict with liberal and pluralist values and inimical to the needs and claims of the poor nations will need to be taken into account. It is true that environmental problems cross frontiers, but it is equally important that they transcend generations. This is significant when we recollect that liberalism does not make of every man or woman an island, although it is true that it is incompatible with the views of a few being imposed on the many. But this latter consideration applies equally to those who wield technological power: to the manufacturers of chemicals that find their way into the food chain and are involuntarily absorbed by newborn babies in their mother's milk, whether that mother is an inhabitant of a developed or a developing nation; to the industrialists whose waste products destroy rivers on which communities have depended; and to governments who opt for energy choices that may create insoluble practical and political problems for future generations. In general, those who have become activists in environmental causes have seen themselves and their families as actually or potentially affected in a very personal and direct way by choices made by others, and over which they have no control. On an issue that is not seen as strictly, narrowly, or purely environmental, the siting of Cruise missiles on Greenham Common, one of the women who initiated the continuing protest there described her motivating insight in terms that very distinctively indicated environmental concern: "I was driving on my way through beautiful scenery in Wales where I live and it suddenly occurred to me how this would all be altered in a nuclear war. And it just stopped me dead in my tracks. I couldn't keep driving. I had to stop and I felt really physically very unwell. And I was crying. I sat for about three quarters of an hour before I could continue the journey."[21]

Similarly, Greenpeace activists who place themselves at risk at the point of radioactive or other poisonous discharges are declaring themselves not as "ecological elitists" but as defenders of individual rights.[22] These rights find this form of expression in the face of the powerlessness created by hierarchical social and political structures in which business and military interests, together with the ambitions and misjudgements of politicians, create apparently irresistible vortices into which ordinary people are swept willy-nilly without consent or consultation.

What applies to individuals in developed societies applies equally to people in countries still aspiring to material prosperity. While improvements in food supply and distribution are clearly in their interest, they will have gained little if these are achieved at the costs to life and health exposed in the environmental debate.

A search for international agreement, then, on what might be interpreted in the broadest sense as principles for living is not inconsistent with a liberal or individualist perspective, nor with the true interests of both North and South. Liberalism, after all, has never been interpreted as involving a right to kill or maim other individuals at will. So the preservation of the environment as a condition of survival could be the first step in securing wider human agreement on moral norms. Once humanity is in harmony with its environment, it may be in a position to retreat back along the scale of moral evolution described by Leopold, this time on a wider and less fragmented basis. Again, when narrowly geographical boundaries have been transcended in the cause of improving humanity's relationship with nature, there can be hope that they may again be transcended to secure a right relationship between individual and society and finally between person and person. In other words, perhaps when humanity has ceased to exploit and torture nature, man will cease to exploit and torture man.

Notes

1. Aldo Leopold, "The Land Ethic," in *A Sand County Almanac* (New York: Oxford University Press, 1949) pp. 244–45.
2. B. Ward and R. Dubos, *Only One Earth: The Care and Maintenance of a Small Planet* (London: Deutsch, 1972), p. 24.
3. A. Rand, *The New Left; the Anti-Industrial Revolution* (New York: Signet Books, 1975), pp. 172–73.
4. R. Carson, *Silent Spring* (Boston: Houghton Mifflin, 1962).
5. D. H. Meadows, et al., *The Limits to Growth* (London: Pan, 1972).
6. H. H. Iltis, quoted in W. H. Murdy, "Anthropocentrism: A Modern Version," in *Ethics and the Environment*, ed. D. Scherer and T. Attig (Englewood Cliffs, N.J.: Prentice-Hall, 1983), p. 16.
7. D. H. Meadows, et al., *The Limits to Growth*, p. 150.
8. F. Hirsch, *Social Limits to Growth* (London: Routledge & Kegan Paul, 1977).
9. J. Passmore, *Man's Responsibility For Nature* (London: Duckworth, 1974).
10. See H. A. McCloskey, *Ecological Ethics and Politics* (Totowa, N.J.: Rowman & Littlefield, 1983).
11. M. Midgley, "Duties Concerning Islands," in R. Elliot, and A. Gare, eds. *Environmental Philosophy* (U.K.: Milton Keynes Open University Press, 1983), pp. 166–81.
12. C. D. Stone, *Should Trees Have Standing? Towards Legal Rights for Natural Objects* (Los Altos, Calif.: William Kaufman, 1974).
13. See G. Berkeley, *Three Dialogues* (London: Everyman, 1954).
14. M. R. Cohen, "Josiah Royce," *New Republic* 8 (1916): 119.
15. R. E. Goodin, "Ethical Principles for Environmental Protection," in Elliot and Gare, *Environmental Philosophy*, pp. 3–20.
16. W. H. Murdy, "Anthropocentrism: A Modern Version," in Scherer and Attig, *Ethics and the Environment*, p. 16.
17. J. B. Callicot, "Animal Liberation: A Triangular Affair," in Scherer and Attig *Ethics and the Environment*, p. 69.
18. R. Routley and V. Routley, "Human Chauvinism and Environmental Ethics," in *Environmental Philosophy*, ed. D. Mannison, M. McRobbie, and R. Routley (Canberra: Research School of Social Sciences, Australian National University, 1980), p. 170.
19. K. Popper, *Objective Knowledge* (London: RKP, 1972).
20. W. Heisenberg, "Rationality in Science and Society," in *Can we Survive our Future?*, ed. G. R. Urban, and M. Glenny (London: Bodley Head, 1971), pp. 84–85. Heisenberg

wrote: "Every time we are able to make a new gadget, we should ask ourselves before embarking on its manufacture: what purpose and whose purposes is it going to serve? It is not true that everything that can be invented ought to be invented or that everything that is technologically feasible should be manufactured and marketed" (Ibid., p. 85).

21. H. Weinreich-Haste, 'Engagement and Commitment; the role of affect in moral reasoning and moral responsibility' in *Zur Bestimmung der Moral*, ed. W. Edelstein and G. Nunner-Winkler (Cologne: Suhrkamp Verlag, 1987).
22. For the use of the terms *ecological elitist*, *ecological platonist*, and *ecological dictators*, see McCloskey, *Ecological Ethics and Politics*, chap. 15.

3
Ethics, Sex and Law.

> *Not even the intercourse of the sexes is exempt from the despotism of positive institution. Law pretends even to govern the indisciplinable wanderings of passion, to put fetters on the clearest deductions of reason, and by appeals to the will, to subdue the involuntary affections of our nature. . . . Love withers under constraint; its very essence is liberty. . . .*
> Shelley, Against Legal Marriage

> *Marriage is something more serious than the pleasure of two people in each other's company; it is an institution which, through the fact that it gives rise to children, forms part of the intimate texture of society, and has an importance far beyond the personal feelings of the husband and the wife.*
> Russell, Marriage and Morals

Which of these two views is correct? Can they be reconciled? Is it the case that for social, economic, and institutional reasons the state must impose through law the rigid structure of marriage conceived as an exclusive sexual relationship? Or should laws regarding personal relationships protect the individual from the encroachments of state and society in the field in which he or she is the only ultimate decision maker? What of the rights of those defenceless satellites of the two primary agents—the children of a marriage? Is it not the function of law to have regard for their interests and, if so, what weighting should it give to these? Is the dependency of women around childbirth and early child raising removed, and their liberty therefore enhanced, if the state rather than an individual man assumes economic and practical responsibility for this phase? Or are there alternatives that avoid female self-immolation without removing individual responsibility for offspring by sharing child care between adults of both sexes? How can one combine stability and flexibility in personal relationships, or are these incompatible demands?

These are large questions with important practical, not merely theoretical, implications. But the facts are well-known and the relevant experience is not the prerogative of an esoteric minority. Hence there is every justification for seeking out the principles that should apply on an *a priori* basis rather than assembling statistics about marriage and divorce, about varieties of sexual experience, or about the comparative life-styles of children from stable family backgrounds, institutions, or single-parent families. It is worth saying, though, that these facts include a change to widespread acceptance of sexual relationships outside marriage, the demise of the asymmetrical approach to male and female sexuality, and a high and increasing divorce rate not entirely dissociated from increased health and longevity, factors that have expanded the life span of marriage for people in the wealthier nations. There have also been highly significant technological changes: in contraceptive methods, in techniques of early abortion, and, most recently, in possibilities of separating the conception and bearing of children entirely from the sex act as a result of the development of techniques of artificial insemination, transfer of ova, embryo storage, and *in vitro* fertilisation. Improvements in the status and situation of illegitimate children have accompanied the spread of the one-parent family as, in some areas and groups, the norm rather than the exception.

In relation to these basic facts, there have been changes in the moral basis for judging such matters, with a shift from an absolutist or principle-based morality to either a purely hedonistic or a utilitarian morality, and a shift in the law that one legal writer has described as comparable in significance to the removal of family law from ecclesiastical to secular courts.

This shift in the law is widely interpreted as a liberalisation of law, placing as it does more and more of the adult individual's life outside the control of the state. Paradoxically, however, it produces as a necessary corollary the state's increasing participation in other aspects of life, as more of the responsibilities traditionally associated with the family are assumed by the state. As the intervention of the law decreases in sexual matters, so it increases in the area of economic and child-related aspects of both formal and informal marriage relationships.

The two most significant areas of this Copernican revolution in the law affecting family relationships have been first, the move to easier divorce, and in particular the shift to no-fault divorce, and second, the removal of distinctions between legitimate and illegitimate children. As far as this last point is concerned, even where no children are involved, there have been a number of judgements recognising the status of what might be called quasi-marital arrangements, so that the law is increasingly discounting technical and formal requirements and recognising what exists *de facto* rather than purely *de jure*. Indeed, in the acceptance of no-fault divorce—divorce based solely on the recognition that a relationship has irretrievably broken down—the law is specifically preferring the recognition of the *de facto* situation, whereas in the past the technical, formal, and *de jure* aspects would have been considered crucial. Added to these changes has been a transformation of sex roles as a result of equal-rights legislation, bringing with it greater economic equality between the sexes.

In general, these legal reforms have come about in response to pressure from public opinion—that is to say, from people not themselves lawyers, philosophers, or professionals, who, nevertheless, have a conception of how they want the world to be. Rigid laws appropriate to different times and conditions are seen as standing in the way of such a conception or ideal, either because they violate intuitively felt moral notions—basic principles of justice expressible as human rights—or because they stand in the way of the happiness of individuals. Both of these are moral conceptions, and it is, as a matter of fact, the case that such moral notions are the mainspring of pressures for legal reform. Questions of the relation between law and morality raise many theoretical problems, but that there is this kind of pragmatic relation provides a reasonable starting assumption. Having made this assumption, though, it will be useful to turn to some consideration of the theoretical background—to the question of the appropriate relation between law and morality where sexual morality is concerned—before turning to the question of alternative underlying ethical approaches.

From a liberal point of view, the personal and private nature of sexual relationships creates a *prima facie* case for minimal legislative control. In contrast, public acts and acts that affect other people against their wishes and without their consent are agreed-upon and obvious areas for social control. So, in most societies, murder and theft have been areas for legal concern and penal sanction. But by these two criteria of publicity and consent, the case for legal and social interference in sexual relationships is slight. Against these considerations, however, must be set the fact that socially and politically, they seldom *have* been free from control. Virtually all societies have created a framework of law and permitted practice to regulate people in the most intimate area of their conduct and behaviour. Indeed, where the key institution of marriage is concerned, some would see the regulations surrounding it as in a very fundamental way defining the culture and essence of a society. For example, Devlin has argued that, as far as British society is concerned, the institution of monogamous marriage is part of the fabric of that society—so much so, that if anyone wishes to live in any other way, then "if he wants to live in the house, he must accept it as built in the way in which it is."[1]

It is interesting to notice the agreement between this establishment position and the claim of radical feminists and Marxists that marriage is part of the political and economic apparatus of capitalist society. These critics of the institution of marriage see it as the keystone of an ideology to which they have given the name "capitalist patriarchy." The term implies a sociological analysis in terms of male domination of the female. This domination is seen as part of a process that guarantees men knowledge of their offspring and so makes possible the acquisition of personal and private property on a generation to generation basis. The radical feminist and the Marxist analysis diverge in the emphasis they place on the importance of fluctuations in economic organisation, particularly where these are seen as a matter of the domination of class by class. Marxists see nonexploitative relations between men and women as being a possibility in a classless society and would claim that exploitation has been largely a consequence of economic factors. Radical feminists, on the other hand, see the exploitation of women by men as a feature common to all the main historic forms of social organisation and therefore something that could continue even within a society organised without traditional class divisions. Some feminists find the only alternative in the notion of matriarchy, and so look back with approval to matriarchal forms of social organisation that existed in earlier periods, usually in relatively primitive and simple forms of society.

These are questions of power and control, and the fact is that in any power struggle between the sexes, fabled Amazons notwithstanding, women have always been handicapped not only by their, on the average, smaller weight and stature than men, but by the unremitting and debilitating cycle of child-bearing and child rearing. Law, being made by men, simply reinforced and institutionalised this physical advantage enjoyed by men, so that physical power, law, and economic strength were able to come together in patriarchal institutions.

Recognising the background of causation though, is not enough on its own to justify in the present day placing a private and domestic relationship at the centre of a legal, social, and economic nexus. Nevertheless, where social causes may be found, social consequences may be expected to follow. This is likely to be admitted where child raising is concerned, since this is more clearly of social and not merely personal concern. And capitalist patriarchy is a notion that is specially concerned with the institution of marriage as a setting for having children and for property arrangements connected with this aim. But there is a case for saying that there are economic and ethical aspects to personal and sexual relationships, apart from the question of children. Even without the complicating factor of child-bearing, powerful attachments are formed between people whose rupture by one partner can lead to breakdown and even inability to survive in the other. People may, on the basis of strong psychological bonds like these, form social or economic units that will need to be taken account of in any welfare or taxation arrangements by a society, if these are to be administered fairly and justly. But then the kind of groupings recognised for these purposes by the state will be the result of a decision that is essentially political and that will give the society that makes it its character and structure. It scarcely needs saying that, for example, a polygamous society and a monogamous society look very different and are very different places to live, and that both are different again from a free-love commune set up in some remote rural retreat. Again, a society that recognises homosexual groupings is going to look very different from one that recognises only orthodox heterosexual relationships.

The aim, common to much legislation, of protecting the individual from hurt, harm, or abuse can, once this point is recognised, easily be extended to the task of providing sign-posts to people in sophisticated societies in which all or most of these things may be the practice of different coexisting groups or individuals. This provides an ethical reason for the intervention of law, but it does not in itself indicate the kind of ethical assumptions that should underly that law. What is the relation, then, between ethics and law, where personal sexual morality is concerned? As far as the latter is concerned, the advent of reliable contraception has changed the basis of the relation between the sexes by producing a radical change in the practical consequences of different patterns of sexual behaviour. Has it also changed it from a moral point of view? The assumption must be that if things *can* be different, then it is also possible that they *ought* to be. But whether, and in what way, is open to discussion.

Some would say that whatever moral conclusions are reached, law and morality remain separate and independent matters, while others would argue that law is based upon and should reflect morality. Between these two opposing viewpoints lies a continuum of possibilities. At one end of the continuum and nearer to the second position is the view that there is something very wrong with a situation in which law enforces what morality forbids or forbids what morality ordains. For the kind of society where this situation prevails obliges its citizens to be saints, martyrs, hypocrites, or quislings—none of these particularly attractive alternatives for the ordinary person disposed to engage in other things in life than political confrontation. Nearer to the first viewpoint, on the other hand, is the liberal notion that law should respect individual autonomy, and that the right to be morally self-determining is one of the most vital of human freedoms. In this respect, the statement in the Universal Declaration of Human Rights that people have a right to privacy in home and family (Article 12) may seem the most pertinent and most relevant where legislation touching on sexual relationships is concerned.

Before legal aspects can be considered, though, the general question must be raised of what *is* the moral basis of sexual relationships. What is the moral court of appeal in which specific and practical ethical issues are to be argued? While many variations in moral outlook can be found, there are certain fundamentally different approaches to ethics that are of particular relevance here.

First, there is the possibility of a wholly selfish ethic—that of egoism, hedonism, or the pursuit of personal gratification, which will be referred to here as personal hedonism. Second, there are approaches based on expediency and the consideration of consequences, in particular consequences that concern happiness, that are, broadly speaking, utilitarian. Third, there are approaches based on appeal to fundamental principles or an irreducible notion of the good. This may be described as principled morality, and in contemporary terms is probably best expressed in terms of human rights; shared values such as freedom, equality, and respect for persons; and ultimate respect for individual autonomy.

Fourth, there is the possibility of basing sexual morality on religious belief. Here it will be taken for granted that religious freedom is a fundamental principle of society and that it should be protected by law. However, there are many religions and many varieties of even the Christian religion. So freedom to conform to religious precepts has to be set alongside broader moral considerations, and in particular against the moral rights of other people. So, in general, and particularly where religious requirements are concerned, somebody's belief that something is a duty is not necessarily a conclusive reason why it should receive the backing of law. That something *is* a duty, on the other hand *is* a good reason. For example, a doctor may for religious reasons believe he has a duty to preserve the life of an eight-day-old foetus against the wishes of a pregnant woman. The law need not support him in this judgement and indeed the legal position varies in different countries. On the other hand, his duty to save the life of an eight-year-old child will be upheld by the law, since all legal systems share his moral perception of the second situation in normal circumstances. Legislation, then does, in fact, presuppose a moral judgement.

Finally, a libertarian position is possible, but as the previous example shows, this must be a qualified position. In particular it must be distinguished from the claim, made by some people, that morality has no part to play in decisions connected with the area of sexuality. This position could be described as the position of the amoralist, since it involves the view that moral considerations could be excluded (a) in deciding personal policy on sexual matters and (b) in judging the behaviour and character of others. It is important to take this point of view seriously, for there would be little point in discussing sexual morality if this rather significant figure in the field of sexual practices were to be excluded from the discussion. However, a closer examination of the amoralist's position will show that this is something of a misdescription, for such a person has in fact very strongly formed views about the rules of sexual behaviour.

The need to make choices, take decisions, even negative ones, imposes itself on every human being, and the difficulty of not conforming to an identifiable pattern is as great as the difficulty of creating a random number series. Very few of those who renounce principles are in fact seeking to adopt random, as opposed to free, behaviour. What they are in fact rejecting is a Kantian ethic—an ethic of fixed principles that involves its holder in sometimes doing what on other grounds he would prefer not to do. In its place they are putting an ethic of one of the first two kinds mentioned, either one of personal gratification or of a more generalised pursuit of happiness. In either case, they are considering the consequences of particular actions to be of more importance than the nature of types of action—immediate judgements about effects rather than rigid adherence to rules. Nevertheless, if an attempt were to be made to outlaw the particular type of sexual behaviour that they prefer, or the pattern into which they thoughtlessly fall, then they would be likely to recognise the nature of the moral claim that they are implicitly making against the rest of society.

Is there, then, a genuinely libertarian position available? The answer to this question must await the rest of this discussion, for libertarianism is not, as the above considerations show, a genuine *moral* option. Morality is, in a sense, bound to be dogmatic, for it involves having a view about what is right, what is good, what is wrong, and what is evil. It therefore makes implicit judgements about the behaviour of others and imposes a pattern on personal decision making. But once this point is accepted, the libertarian stance on sexual behaviour acquires content and meaning in relation to the wider libertarian position. On the whole, the libertarian wishes to avoid pressuring other people and the pressure of others on himself or herself. But the libertarian in the sexual field is not committed to the view that any type of sexual behaviour is as good as any other. His view, or hers, is essentially a view about the limits of law and social interference. But before saying more than this, it will be worth looking more closely at the options that have already been mentioned.

Personal Hedonism

Does personal hedonism, or the pursuit of personal gratification, provide an adequate ethical basis for sexual behaviour? In moral philosophy in general, it is widely agreed that this theory does not provide an adequate basis for ethics—for determining, that is, the whole range of social and interpersonal conduct. But people who would accept this might still think that in the narrower field of sexual behaviour, it does provide an adequate base, and indeed the ideal base. The wider ethical discussion involves distinguishing first of all the theory known as psychological hedonism from what is usually called ethical egoism. Psychological hedonism is an ethical theory only by implication, for it is the psychological theory that people *can* only act in pursuit of their own pleasure and to minimise their own pain. In this sense it is a deterministic theory that leaves no room for morality. But ethical egoism, which in this context it is preferable to describe as personal hedonism, avoids the psychological judgement and is more justifiably regarded as an ethical viewpoint because it is the judgement that this is the only ground on which people *ought* to act. On the other hand, this formulation of the theory reveals its fundamental weakness. It is essentially impossible to put it forward as a general moral theory—as a theory that is about what "people" ought to do—because of the logical difficulty of generalising egoism. What *does* the egoist say about what other people ought to do? Pursue his (i.e., the egoist's) happiness? Or each pursue his own? But that is an altruistic recommendation, the making of which would run counter to the basic position.

So egoism, or personal hedonism, is flawed as a general ethical position by an inescapable logical incoherence. This general defect, then, will inevitably carry over into the particular application of the theory in the area of sexual behaviour. But here there are more substantial difficulties of a moral rather than a purely logical kind. The theory necessarily involves using other people as a means to personal gratification if, as is usually the case, the personal hedonist's sexual tastes include activities involving other people. It also involves risks to the hedonist himself or herself, since if the recommendation to pursue personal gratification is generalised and everyone uses it as a guide to behaviour, then this creates a Hobbesian sexual state of "war of every man against every man" but also against every woman, and vice versa. But, of course, where sexual relationships are concerned, it is very often not only adult participants who are involved but also children. That their interests need to be given special consideration outside the framework of the personal gratification of adults is a principle supported both by arguments of a paternalistic nature and by arguments in support of the consideration of the interests of others. Both of these arguments will be considered later. Meantime it is clear that there are serious defects in personal hedonism as an ethical theory appropriate for the area of sexual behaviour.

Utilitarianism

Although utilitarianism is the name of a much more widely respected ethical theory that it is impossible to consider here in its full form, it is a term that can usefully sum up an approach to the more limited area of sexual morality based on seeking the happiest outcome for those concerned. But the very limitation "for those concerned" points to an immediate difficulty in this point of view. If the phrase is meant to cover society as a whole, then this is by no means a simple calculation. But if only those directly affected are to be considered, then the problem arises that marriage, in fact, provides a test case for this form of utilitarianism. This is because an essential aspect of marriage is that it is based on the idea of an early promise overriding later inclination or expediency.

Divorce figures today show an increasing willingness on the part of individuals to choose personal happiness in preference to the routine continuance of obligations, but this may be more a demonstration of a swing to the personal hedonist outlook rather than the utilitarian. For the utilitarian point of view does involve taking into account the balance of happiness to more individuals than the central agent. There is, for instance, the unhappiness of the deserted spouse where the decision is not a mutual one, that of children, and indeed of other relatives. There could even be an effect on the immediate community where imitative behaviour is precipitated by example. So it is much less clear than might at first appear to be the case what even a simple and narrow utilitarian calculation would entail in relation to the institution of marriage, and what the happiness effects of alternatives to marriage are.

Utility must also be limited as a ground for legislation for other reasons. Laws against miscegenation or homosexuality could make a majority of people happy in a particular society but would conflict with the moral rights or claims of individuals. For these reasons, then, utilitarianism can scarcely provide a sole or complete basis for sexual morality.

Principled Morality

For this view, we may look both to the secular or philosophically minded intuitionist and also to the religious believer whose religion gives explicit guidance on the subject of sexual behaviour. At this stage it will not be necessary to distinguish these different grounds for a fixed-principle morality, although clearly, religious believers base their principles on authority and revelation, while intuitionists believe in the self-evidence of their principles and their accessibility to rational recognition or discovery. Intuitionists are most likely to compare the discovery of moral truth to the discovery of mathematical truth and to see both as ultimately beyond further justification.

An immediate charge likely to be made against this type of view is that it is too rigid in practice. History and literature have made us more aware than previous generations of the human misery resulting from the harsh application of principles untempered by compromise, in those intimate and private areas where emotions and feeling rule. One principle in particular has already been mentioned as being of special significance here and that is the principle of promise keeping. But promises concerning personal relationships are exceptional because they could be said to involve a commitment to what is outside the promisor's control—a situation that would in all other cases be held to invalidate a promise. You cannot, for example, promise to give somebody someone else's house, nor can you marry if you are already married, even if you go through the formal marriage ceremony. It is and always has been the rule, though, for people to promise to *remain* married, and while they can certainly remain married in name, certain kinds of personal feeling can make a marriage relationship impossible. So while Victorian morality would have demanded the technical continuance of the relationship under virtually any circumstances, the law now recognises that a marriage in name only is no longer a marriage. As a result, this may place the ending of a marriage beyond the control of either partner, since sexual and emotional satisfaction are not necessarily matters under conscious control.

Secondly, principles governing relationships are exceptional in another respect as well. While it is the hallmark of moral principles that they are universal in their application, principles in this area are necessarily particular and specific. The essence of these principles is that they involve special obligations to particular individuals. It may, though, be possible to account for these special features without invalidating the general notion of principles as being important for the ethics of sexual relationships. In particular, broad principles that apply in other areas as well play a part here that is not essentially different from the part they play in relation to other aspects of human life. These are principles such as fairness, consideration of others, lack of exploitation, honesty, openness and the degree of commitment involved in intending to keep a promise.

The Libertarian View

Returning to the libertarian viewpoint, it will be clear that for libertarians who have succeeded in separating their position from that of the amoralist, elements of all the previous moral positions are relevant to the claims they wish to make politically and socially. A morality of fixed principles will be comprehensible and justifiable to someone whose position is itself defined in terms of principle. Libertarians are characterised by the fact that they are prepared to recognise in freedom an ultimate and absolute principle. They will not, therefore, be unsympathetic to the claims of those who assert other principles of this kind, although they will wish to press the claims of freedom in cases of conflict. Some degree of utilitarian calculation, though, may also play a part in the libertarian position, since it is a part of that position to insist that no harm be done to one individual by another. Therefore, restrictions as far as the happiness of others and the welfare of children are concerned must enter into this position. Finally, since many people will want or use freedom in order to pursue personal happiness where other considerations do not exclude this, the libertarian is in no sense the enemy of the personal hedonist, and, indeed, personal hedonists will no doubt find the libertarian stance the most congenial to their own position.

Nevertheless, there are serious difficulties in identifying a basic libertarian position and in particular in separating it from a liberal position. It is most readily understood as a demand for freedom from regulation in one's private life, but in the special area of sexual relationships the liberal's desire to resist totalitarianism in the sense of state domination of the life of the individual seems to conflict with the demand, potentially totalitarian in its consequences, for the state to take over the traditional role of the family. In particular, feminist demands for *female* freedom may run counter to traditional liberal demands for a reduction in the involvement of state agencies in personal and private life. In this case, the price paid for the freedom of one sex may be too high if bought at the cost of important freedoms of both sexes. Given the permanent tendency of human beings to construct hierarchies of power, and given pressures for conformity, the value of institutions that cut across political, economic, and social hierarchies is inestimable. Of these institutions, the family as a biological and natural network must be one of the most powerful. It is striking that this aspect of the role of the family was alluded to by Russell at a time when the contemporary decline in the fortunes of the family could hardly have been foreseen. In *Marriage and Morals*, he wrote: "If the State were to adopt the role of the father, the State would, *ipso facto*, become the sole capitalist. Thoroughgoing Communists have often maintained the converse, that if the State is to be the sole capitalist, the family, as we have known it, cannot survive."[2]

Whichever way round best expresses the truth, the fact is that any totalitarian scheme, starting with that of Plato's *Republic*, seems necessarily to involve the elimination of the family as a source of subversion. The invisible bonds it creates between its members give rise to loyalties that purely artificial structures based on political, economic, or even military systems of organisation cannot without great difficulty override. Both the Israeli kibbutzim and the Russian experiments of the post-Revolution period were attempts to cut across family relationships in order to bind together individual members of either a local or statewide enterprise. In Germany in the 1930s and in Orwell's 1984, as in China under the Red Guards, organisations for young people attempted to provide another form of loyalty bonding in which children were encouraged to monitor the political conformity of their parents and, if necessary, denounce them to the authorities. A libertarian, then, if a true lover of liberty, may need to keep a wary eye on the political consequences of freedom in personal relationships, if the consequence of this freedom is the atomisation of society—the creation of the rootless and anomic individual, free of love, loyalty, and commitment.

Nevertheless, a retreat into fixed, unchanging roles and class and family structures is neither feasible nor desirable. Today's requirement is for principles of behaviour adapted to a world in which these ancient simplicities can no longer hold sway. William Godwin, a philosophical opponent of marriage, once wrote: "The supposition that I must have a companion for life is the result of a complication of vices. It is the dictate of cowardice, and not of fortitude. It flows from the desire of being loved and esteemed for something that is not desert."[3] Similarly, Shelley, who was an admirer of Godwin's political and social views, wrote of "the despotism of marriage" and "the fanatical ideal of chastity," which he described as a monkish and evangelical superstition striking at the root of all domestic happiness. "How long," he asked, "ought the sexual connection to last? What law ought to specify the extent of the grievances which should limit its duration?" And his reply was: "A husband and wife ought to continue so long united as they love each other; any law which should bind them to cohabitation for one moment after the decay of their affection would be a most intolerable tyranny, and the most unworthy of toleration."[4]

It is at this point that the distinction between the personal and the political becomes most pressing. But that society should ultimately insist on the continuation of a union in which the "decay of affection" has irretrievably occurred is no longer even an issue at law. The "odour of sanctity" suggested by Santayana as some compensation at this stage in a marriage has become distasteful rather than venerable. Santayana wrote: "In fortunate cases love may glide imperceptibly into settled domestic affections, giving them a touch of ideality; for when love dies in the odour of sanctity people venerate his relics."[5] Santayana, however, recognised sex as "nature's categorical imperative" and made no claims about the inevitability of preserving the domestic situation in its traditional form. For he went on to say that "man . . . is polygamous by instinct, although often kept faithful by habit no less than by duty, . . ." and with distinctive penetration remarked: "To be omnivorous is one pole of true love: to be exclusive is the other."[6]

On a personal level, then, there may be conflict between two kinds of ideals: between the ideal of exclusivity and the ideal of variety; and between the ideal of permanence or long-term loyalty and the facts of change and the transitoriness of all aspects of human life, not least the aspect of love and affection. Indeed, that there should be a direct relationship between intensity and impermanence where emotion and attachment are concerned may be, other than in exceptional cases, something to be accepted as one of the sad inevitabilities of the human lot. But, again on the personal level, where the social context is ignored, a sacrifice of intensity and delight to lukewarm prolongation of a relationship would have limited appeal. Santayana, having spoken of "settled domestic affections," also wrote convincingly of the delights of a more intense form of association, describing in vivid terms

> the joy of gazing on the beloved, of following or being followed, of tacit understandings and avowals, of flight together into some solitude to people it with those ineffable confidences which so naturally follow the outward proofs of love. All this makes the brightest page of many a life, the only bright page in the thin biography of a many a human animal, while if the beasts could speak they would give us, no doubt, endless versions of the only joy in which, as we may fancy, the blood of the universe flows consciously through their hearts.[7]

Again, on a personal level, to sacrifice such joys for empty formal arrangements might seem to mean losing, if Santayana is right, part of the point and sensation of being alive. But to be continually buffeted to and fro between these two poles, trapped within these dichotomies, is a fundamental feature of human existence—at least when reflection on life succeeds to unreflective engagement with it. It is also an acute form of the fundamental ethical dilemma, in which Kantian rigour in sticking to principle whatever the practical consequences is constantly in conflict with teleological calculation of ends and utilities.

But in this particular case, it may be that the starker choice can, after all, be avoided. For to sacrifice the promiscuous and ephemeral pursuit of Santayana's "only joy" is not necessarily to sacrifice all variety, change, and development in sexual and emotional relationships. And the enrichment of life and personal involvements that this implies are not necessarily incompatible with—indeed they may demand—a keener acceptance of the responsibility and self-denial that result from voluntarily allowing oneself to become a focus of others' expectations and dependency.

What is needed, then, of a new sexual ethic is this: it needs to recognise jealous exclusivity for the personally and socially damaging characteristic it in fact is. It needs to preserve the gains made in sexual parity in employment and status. It should not be based on any expectation of sacrificing some people's sexual fulfilment on the altar of sexual conformity (for example, by limiting the civil rights of homosexuals). But it needs to achieve these things without contributing to an erosion of the family structure by creating a vacuum to be filled by expanding and encroaching agencies of the state.

Are these compromises possible? It is only in a liberal state that they would be attempted, or could be thought desirable. They constitute a test of the adaptability of the human spirit and of its willingness to retain what is valuable in human relations without a deadening ossification of morality. What is undoubtedly true is that unless a liberal ideology and the liberal society can unite these contradictions and resolve the tensions they create, embodying a new consensus in law and social institutions, that society is likely to survive only long enough to witness its own disintegration.

Notes

1. P. Devlin, *The Enforcement of Morals* (Oxford: Oxford University Press, 1965), p. 9.
2. B. Russell, *Marriage and Morals* (London: Allen & Unwin, 1972), p. 9–10.
3. R. M. Wardle, ed., *Godwin and Mary: Letters of William Godwin and Mary Wollstonecraft* (Lawrence: University of Kansas Press, 1967), pp. 92, 102. Quoted in D. Locke, *A Fantasy of Reason* (London: Routledge & Kegan Paul, 1980), p. 129.
4. P. B. Shelley, "Against legal Marriage," in *Shelley on Love*, ed. Richard Holmes (London: Anvil Press Poetry, 1980), p. 45.
5. G. Santayana, *The Life of Reason*, bk. 2, *Reason in Society* (London: Constable, 1905), pp. 33–34.
6. Ibid., pp. 22, 25.
7. Ibid., pp. 15–16.

4
The Limits of Toleration

Respect for freedom of conscience is widely held to be a virtue. Against this virtue, however, must be set the vice of tolerating the intolerable. According to a certain view of conscience, this conflict would never arise because it would be held that conscience never can lead astray: the deliverances of conscience are always right. But this would mean attributing a great deal of implausible insincerity to other people and would suggest a coincidence of moral opinion that seems as a matter of fact to be far from the truth. The most superficial acquaintance with varieties of opinion in culture, in class, and in different societies suggests that the phenomenon that we describe as conscience can yield strikingly different results when consulted by, for example, a tribesman in Papua New Guinea, a Chinese villager, or a cosmopolitan New Yorker or Londoner.

It follows that sometimes what people believe passionately that they ought to do will cut diametrically across what others believe they ought to do. For those who believe in imposing their view of what ought to be on others willy-nilly, or irrespective of what those people believe or want, this will present no more than a practical problem. But for those who include as one of their most cherished convictions a belief in the right of all to self-determination, to the unhindered pursuit of their chosen way of life, their freedom to think for themselves and choose for themselves, sooner or later difficult conflicts will arise.

This is inherent in the notion of toleration itself. For to tolerate what one does not object to is neither difficult in practice, nor, strictly speaking, conceivable in logic. The true test of toleration and the exact force of its meaning emerge only when what is to be tolerated is something that one would object to on every other ground.

The toleration principle itself has an ethical, a social, and a politico-legal form. And the limits of toleration may be set differently according to which version is in question. Even in its ethical form, however, it does not amount to: "X is right where X is any opinion or practice anyone conscientiously espouses." Setting aside for present purposes the question of whether an acceptable form of the ethical version can be found;[1] the socio-legal principle of toleration of opinion may be loosely formulated as:

1. "If X is an opinion that is sincerely held by someone, then neither law nor public opinion should attempt to suppress it."

However, the social and the legal may be readily separated and the question of practical toleration incorporated by the following expansions.

2. *The Social Principle.* "If X is an opinion or practice that is sincerely held/believed obligatory by someone, then X should not be openly morally censured by others although they may tacitly condemn it. They may not apply the social sanctions of avoidance or overtly expressed distaste that may be open to them."

3. *The Politico-legal Principle.* "If X is an opinion or practice that is sincerely held/believed obligatory by someone, then X should be legally permitted and the institutional structure of society (e.g., arrangements within education or health care) should be arranged to accommodate them."

As so expressed, there are certain relatively easy test cases for the toleration principle in all its forms, at least from the moderate liberal standpoint of Western democracy. These might well be sexual behaviour, individual life-style where this has little effect on other people, and religious observance in the case of moderate mainstream religions.

But the topic under consideration here is the limits of toleration, and it is clear that these limits are reached when the toleration principle itself comes into conflict with other deeply felt moral norms. Three cases in particular provide striking illustrations of this point. Two of these have aroused recent public controversy within the United Kingdom, and they result particularly from the intermingling of cultures and traditions in a single society, that of Britain in the 1980s. The third is both a more widespread and a more endemic issue with roots that go back as far as Western cultural traditions can be traced. They are:

1. *Treatment of and Attitudes to Women under Moslem Religion.* We may, for example, as an extreme instance, consider the practice of female circumcision, which may, in some parts of the world, meet with the acceptance, indeed the moral fervour, of all concerned. Or the practice of arranged marriages, and restrictions on the educational, public, or professional life of women and girls.

2. *The Halal Meat Issue*. This is the issue of the religious slaughter of animals according to the tenets of both Moslem and Jewish religions—techniques that involve slaughter without prestunning and that may or may not cause fear and pain in the animal. Again, however, it is an important moral and religious article of faith that this practice should be observed.

3. *The Racism Issue*. This is the issue of racism as an ideology—the naked phenomenon of racial hatred must be set aside here as beyond the scope of this discussion. The legal step, in Great Britain, of banning the expression of racist views adds a further dimension to the issue. Since racism as an ideology is often a feature of a wider extremist political position, this example might be taken to extend to the more general issue of the holding of widely hated extremist political opinions, particularly where these would themselves involve repression of opinion and intolerance. A particular and acute form of this controversy occurs when racist or totalitarian views are signalled by an individual's membership of extremist organisations, and the following two questions arise: (1) Should that person be socially tolerated, for example, in an educational or employment setting? and (2) should that membership and that organisation be legally sanctioned?

These are some of the questions that prompt the reflections that follow. For many people, the three cases cited will test their conception of the limits of toleration—this against a background in which to the general question "Must one tolerate the intolerable?" a powerful ethical lobby now says no. In political life generally, the notion of toleration is becoming outmoded on the left and brushed aside impatiently on the right, where a quiet beating-up on a dark night may be seen as the best way to deal with offensive opinions; while for extremists of both persuasions, political assassination and physical violence are openly advocated as efficacious supplanters of persuasion and argument. With self-conscious bias, Marcuse, in *Repressive Tolerance*, advocated "intolerance against movements from the Right and toleration of movements from the Left."[2] He advocated this radical notion of "liberating tolerance" as a replacement for the liberal or conventional notion of tolerance as something that embraces all views. Meanwhile, outside the realms of philosophical discussion, an American president was recently embarrassed in his campaign for reelection by the discovery of a CIA manual on assassination circulated in Nicaragua for use against leftist leaders.

Does the notion of toleration, then, need to be reappraised? Are both left and right here to be found with a clearer perception of utilitarian necessity, if not of truth and virtue, than the old liberal advocates of the open society? Is pluralism merely an empty shell, with tolerance a part of that dead husk?

In order to answer these questions, it is necessary first of all to recognise and understand the function of some ambiguities in the notion of toleration of opinion. As a preliminary, it is first necessary to consider its relation to the notion of tolerating the *expression* of an opinion. This might seem to be a reasonably straightforward notion even if there is dispute about precisely where censorship rather than freedom of utterance and of publication should apply.

But expressing an opinion may be more or less passive, more or less aggressive. At the aggressive end of the continuum, messianic proselytizing is clearly in the public domain, as is incitement to action (racial harrassment, for example), while at the passive end of the spectrum, expressing an opinion shades into the mere holding of an opinion, and opinion that is silently held and never divulged is beyond social or legal control. But if the person concerned is not prepared to lie, then direct questioning—or a demand that he declare himself against an opinion or perform some act that is inconsistent with the opinion, such as participating in a religious or political ceremony—will bring that private commitment into the public realm. If this counts as the expression of opinion, then the distinction between holding and expressing an opinion is ineluctably eroded.

Opinion, too, may be shaped by education, propaganda, or mass advertising. And if opinion is not, after all, immutable, then the protection of a right to an opinion may not be ultimately distinguishable from the protection of a right to its expression. Those who have most forcefully pointed out this connection have not necessarily done so in order to draw a liberal inference. Marcuse, for example, uses the social influences on opinion as part of his ammunition against liberal toleration. He writes:

> Tolerance toward that which is radically evil now appears as good because it serves the cohesion of the whole on the road to affluence or more affluence. The toleration of the systematic moronisation of children and adults alike by publicity and propaganda, the release of destructiveness in aggressive driving, the recruitment for and training of special forces, the impotent and benevolent tolerance toward outright deception in merchandizing, waste, and planned obsolescence are not distortions and abberations, they are the essence of a system which fosters tolerance as a means for perpetuating the struggle for existence and suppressing the alternatives.[3]

Marcuse is correct in pointing out that opinion is not merely a matter of utterance or expression but may form part of a whole way of life. But what follows from this close connection must be considered in the wider context created by the notion of action as flowing from opinion and embodied in expression. First, though, it must be said that the ambiguities in the notion of toleration of opinion have not been fully exposed when its links with the issue of expression of opinion have been brought to light. A second ambiguity arises from the fact that opinion, even unstated and uncommunicated, has a value in itself that is entirely dependent on its truth, accuracy, reasonableness, and moral respect-worthiness. This—which may be called its truth value—is quite distinct from the value of that opinion in the world of affairs, and indeed may not even coincide with its usefulness. (Take, for example, the utter counter productiveness of establishing *any* truth about racial differences, whether these are flattering or demeaning to the race in question—recognised superiority, after all, is as much a recipe for resentment as is recognised inferiority.) The ambiguity in question here consists, then, in the fact that talk of tolerating an opinion can be interpreted as attributing truth value to it, or at least as failing to repudiate it. But of course, there can be no virtue in tolerating a worthless or immoral opinion in any sense that carries with it endorsement of that opinion. This sort of endorsement would be a betrayal of what one believes oneself.

So there is a sense in which opinion itself can never be tolerated, since if one shares the opinion, it makes no sense to speak of tolerating it, and if one disagrees with it, then one is committed to its repudiation. But opinions do not arrive in the world ownerless and unparented. They come only attached to people, and are, moreover, seldom divorced from actions. There is, then, a validity attached to the notion of toleration of opinion as a social phenomenon, attached to a person and issuing in action, that is missing from the notion of opinion alone, stark and unembodied in its social context. This might seem to reverse one's initial intuition—according to which a disembodied consequence-free opinion is more easily tolerated—but from the point of view of religious believers, for example, it is not enough that their sincerely held beliefs should be formulable or that they should not be molested for holding them; they must also be able to live by the precepts and customs of their religion. Here, where belief expresses itself concretely in the world, the question of toleration becomes one of social and legal sanctions, institutional arrangements, punishment and control.

These considerations make the justification of toleration more difficult, since arguments for toleration have usually involved attempting to separate moral opinion from physical action by one criterion or another. The attempt to separate law and morality by means of a distinction between public and private goes back at least to J. S. Mill's demarcation between matters that concern only the individual and matters that affect others. In a much cited passage, Mill wrote: "The only part of the conduct of any one, for which he is amenable to society, is that which concerns others.... Over himself, over his own mind and body, the individual is sovereign."[4] In his reference to "mind," Mill clearly placed the holding of opinions within the private, rather than public, domain.

But the roots of the idea of a private domain could be held to lie in the biblical injunction to "Render unto Caesar the things which are Caesar's and to God the things which are God's"—an injunction that although often given the contrary interpretation, in fact sets the individual conscience against the demands of the state and of law. The Wolfenden Report on prostitution and homosexuality gave legal effect to this essentially philosophical principle in the memorable assertion that some parts of life are "not the law's business," and it recommended a situation in which both prostitution and homosexuality were to be tolerated if practiced away from the public eye. Where such a distinction can be maintained, practical toleration may, indeed, need no further justification. But the cases cited here are distinguished by the fact that they offer no such possible solution. This is because concern for the defenceless—for women and girls in a sexually closed society, for animals in the unquiet privacy of the abbatoir—is not assuaged by the invisibility of the evil complained of. And racism is felt to be a pervading evil in a similar way—an evil which cannot, except in the short term, be taken to be free of practical consequences for a minority group who may need the protection and active vigilance of the majority.

The question, then, is whether these cases create a special problem as far as belief and action are concerned, or whether the inseparability of the two is not the standard feature in relation to most important beliefs. And first it must be said that the *triviality* of the belief is no measure of its relationship to action. If beliefs about trivial matters are not worth enquiring about, then that is only because they are not worth the paper or the breath, not because they provide a line of demarcation between belief and action. Once this point is noticed, it becomes clear that most of the beliefs we consider important are actually beliefs *about* action. If we take the standard case for toleration, religious belief, it is only at the most superficial level that it can be taken as a case of abstract and metaphysical belief without consequences in the real world. Religion has always been potentially subversive, and in spite of the long history of the establishment of religion as part of the apparatus of the state, it has repeatedly thrown up martyrs, saints, heroes, and dissidents who have posed a challenge to the body politic.

Moral beliefs and opinion are again only superficially to be considered abstract rather than action-guiding. In particular, moral belief in human rights or in a transcendent natural law plainly sets the individual judgement against all but a morally well-grounded law and administration. And if we take the case of political beliefs, since these are most frequently at issue in controversies about toleration, quite clearly *politics* is a term that conspicuously covers a broad spectrum of action rather than opinion. Political answers are answers to the question "what is to be done?" Very often in political matters the possibilities reduce to two that are pure contradictions. Either there would be Cruise missiles on Greenham Common or not. On such matters of crucial importance, no liberal consensus, no middle course, is possible.

But perhaps toleration of belief could be separated from the question of practice at least in relation to the search for scientific truth? A free exchange of opinion on matters of fact might seem to be a prime case for toleration. For the mere assemblage of facts, it might be thought, leaves everything open as far as action is concerned, action itself being necessarily a consequence of a judgement framed in terms of value rather than of fact. Thus it might be argued that at least in the case of scientific enquiries and matters of fact in general, the expression of opinion can be separated from action. But facts are not dumb clutter strewn meaninglessly about the attic of the world. In their selection, discussion, and bringing into focus they are inevitably acted upon. They are used as stepping-stones to another level of enquiry and are inextricably intermeshed with action.

The notion of pure opinion, then, is better set aside in favour of a more sophisticated awareness and acceptance of the part that opinion, whether religious, moral, political, scientific, or purely factual plays in human affairs. But having rejected this possible criterion of demarcation, it is important to consider what might be offered in its place. One historically important suggestion for this alternative focus, then, is that it is to be found, not in the relation of the opinion to action, but in the relation of the opinion to truth.

Those who oppose toleration may do so on the grounds that where truth is attainable, or is the object of an enquiry, there can be no case for tolerating falsehood. Mill considered this argument also, and his reply to it was that if we are not prepared to tolerate falsehood, then we are assuming our own infallibility. Another and related answer may be possible today in the light of more recent approaches to the philosophy of science and to epistemology. This is that the notion of immutably established truth is foreign to the idea of scientific enquiry itself. As Popper and Kuhn have argued, the search for advances in science is more a matter of conjectures and refutations, of paradigms accepted and rejected, than of certainty, proof, and even irreversible disproof.

But questions of subjective certainty and conviction, together with these related epistemological questions of the possibility of establishing objective standards of truth and public acceptability, have accompanied the toleration debate from its origins in religious persecution, and it is illuminating to see what solutions were offered in the context of these historic debates about right belief and revelation, about conscience and the light of reason. In the context of the burning of heretics and wars of religion in sixteenth- and seventeenth-century Europe, it was possible to find people giving expression to a number of different arguments for toleration.

1. *Religious truth is a development—a gradual evolution in which people over generations come closer to truth without ever arriving at a position of final unarguable dogma.* This view was expressed by Faustus Socinus who was burned for heresy in Poland in 1604; and the generous nature of his toleration was expressed by the Socinians who succeeded him in a Catechism in which they wrote: "In composing this Catechism we give no order to anyone. In expressing our opinion, we oppress nobody. Let everyone be free to express his judgement in religious matters, provided we too be allowed to express our opinion on all things without injury or insult. . . . In so far as we are concerned we are all brothers, and no power, no authority has been given us over the conscience of the others."[5]

2. *Falsehood is harmless because truth will always triumph.* On this, Milton wrote in his *Areopagitica* (1644), "Let Truth and Falsehood grapple; who ever knew Truth put to the worse, in a free and open encounter?"

3. *In practice, truth cannot be imposed by force.* Luther, before he became as zealously intolerant as others, wrote of the imperviousness of heresy to compulsion: "One cannot strike it with iron, nor burn in with fire." This was in answer to the doctrine indicated by the Latin phrase *compelle intrare*, itself a reference to the parable in which it is urged that those who are reluctant to feast should be "compelled to come in," an admonition taken by some to sanction burning of heretics.

4. *Reason is to be preferred to revelation, even if this entails scepticism about the ability of human beings to attain certainty or truth.* Pierre Bayle adopted this point of view, linking it with the unqualified assertion that "the conscience which is in error has the same rights as that which is not."[6]

5. *Liberty in general is impossible without liberty of conscience.* On this, James Harrington wrote that "a Government pretending to Liberty and yet suppressing Liberty of Conscience, must be a contradiction."[7]

For today, a variety of religious believers may have to choose between a position like that expressed in the 1832 Encyclical of Pope Gregory XVI, which described liberty of conscience as a "delirium" flowing from the foul well of indifferentism, and the more recent position of the Catholic and most other Christian churches, that favours toleration of religious belief despite a continued claim to truth, at least as far as the essentials of the Christian position are concerned.

But these are not only problems for the religious. Any commitment to truth or principle carries with it a necessary unwillingness to concede simultaneously the possibility of error. It is hard to avoid the pitfall of indifferentism when tolerating difference. It may seem that the choices posed as far as toleration is concerned are either to abandon conviction and thus concede the case for toleration on the grounds of uncertainty, or to retain one's convictions at the expense of toleration. The toleration question, however, is whether, on the contrary, it is possible to be committed to the notions (a) that truth is attainable, and (b) that others must still be protected in their errors.

Marcuse's attack on toleration, which was referred to earlier, by-passes this question by reversing the usual notions of truth and falsity. Current views of true and false, right and wrong, are attributed to indoctrination by media and education, themselves the instruments of economic and political power. Likewise, language itself and the words we use are denounced—with a ritual bow to Orwell—as being instruments in this process of indoctrination. Marcuse writes: "Universal toleration becomes questionable when its rationale no longer prevails, when tolerance is administered to manipulated and indoctrinated individuals who parrot as their own, the opinion of their masters, for whom heteronomy has become autonomy."[8]

Marcuse has become so much the symbol of this contemporary viewpoint and the political movements which give it expression that it is difficult to remember that he was himself born less than forty years after the publication of Mill's seminal defence of toleration in *On Liberty*. Mill's argument seems to have influenced Marcuse's thought only negatively in his denunciation of freedom (of opinion, of assembly, of speech) as "an instrument for absolving servitude." In his denunciation of liberal democracy, however, Marcuse provides a reminder, if one were needed, of the close connection between the ideal of tolerance and the ideal of pluralism.

This latter ideal is, however, instrumental in separating the issue of toleration from the question of truth. For if a plurality of views are to flourish, it holds almost as a matter of necessity that falsity must be represented as well as truth. Societies in which a plurality of attitudes and life-styles have flourished have invariably valued the notion of tolerance. In ancient Athens, the statesman Pericles, in his famous funeral oration juxtaposed these two ideals (of pluralism and toleration) in describing Athenian democracy, saying: "There is no exclusiveness in our public life, and in our private intercourse. We are not suspicious of one another, nor angry with our neighbour if he does what he likes; we do not put on sour looks at him, which, though harmless, are not pleasant."[9]

And Plato, describing the same situation unsympathetically, wrote: "Here you are not obliged to be in authority, however competent you may be, or to submit to authority, if you do not like it; you need not fight when your fellow-citizens are at war, nor remain at peace when they do, unless you want peace."[10]

Mill added his own defence of the value of eccentricity and genius, saying, "As it is useful that while mankind is imperfect there should be different opinions, so it is that there should be different experiments in living."[11] On the other hand, the challenge from Marcuse echoes Plato's attack in its tone:

> All points of view can be heard: the Communist and the Fascist, the Left and the Right, the white and the Negro, the crusaders for armament and for disarmament. Moreover, in endlessly dragging debates over the media the stupid opinion is treated with the same respect as the intelligent one, the misinformed may talk as long as the informed, and propaganda rides along with education, truth with falsehood. This pure toleration of sense and nonsense is justified by the democratic argument that nobody, neither group nor individual, is in possession of the truth and capable of defining what is right and wrong, good and bad.[12]

Clearly Marcuse draws the same conclusion as his co-author, R. P. Wolff, that "we must give up the image of society as a battleground of competing groups and formulate an ideal of society more exalted than the mere acceptance of opposed interests and diverse customs. There is a need for a new philosophy of community beyond pluralism and beyond tolerance"[13]

Beyond pluralism and beyond tolerance, however, lies familiar territory from the past—persecution, pogroms, and judicial murder—rather than the heady unexplored vistas implied in Wolff's stirring appeal. The novelty is that here a claim to a monopoly of truth is combined with a denial of the very validity of the notion of truth. For those who attach some meaning to the notion of objectivity, a prime function of toleration is to protect both reason and conscience as agents in the search for truth. But if truth is unattainable, then this is a search for a will-o-the-wisp—the pot of gold at the end of the rainbow. The question of whether it may not sometimes be politic to sacrifice truth cannot even arise if there is no such thing, nor can the question of whether error should be allowed to flourish. As another writer on toleration has said: "The toleration principle is directly put in question at any time it is supposed that there is a truth, that it can be known, and that it enjoys some highest priority or supreme value."[14]

But while truth as a metaphysical abstraction or unqualified and ultimate category may be a disputable concept, the fact is that opinions may be closer to or further from the truth, as well as ethically better or worse, and logically more or less soundly based. In Hannah Arendt's words: "Conceptually, we may call truth what we cannot change; metaphorically, it is the ground on which we stand and the sky that stretches above us."[15]

This is not the kind of objectivity that goes with bigotry and narrow prejudice—rather it is a more qualified assertion of truth or objectivity of the kind that Putnam has described as "objectivity for us." But even a muted belief in ethical or epistemological objectivity may combine with awareness of the facts of what humans do indeed believe—things sometimes outrageous, often improbable, and frequently damaging to the interests of others—to justify our unease when forced to tread the borders of toleration.

We may now return to the three cases cited at the outset, searching for solutions in the light of (a) a commitment to the notion that conviction on both the moral and the factual front is justifiable and appropriate, and (b) a belief that the case for not institutionalising one particular view of truth but allowing a plurality of views to flourish is both pragmatically and morally justified—two requirements that could more picturesquely be summed up as the beliefs (a) that heresy should not flourish and (b) that we should nevertheless no longer burn heretics.

This is on the one hand to advocate the emphatic denunciation of falsity and evil, and, on the other, to insist on the importance of standing back, listening to others, and not attempting coercion. It means resisting bad opinion with good, false opinion with true, and restraining only the person who will not respect these limits himself.

In other words, we are driven to return, in considering the three cases that were cited to begin with, to the question of disembodied opinion. It has been argued here that for all essential purposes, opinion always is embodied and that we therefore have no choice but to separate our attitude to and treatment of the person from our attitude to and treatment of the opinion.

In the contemporary world, both the state-sanctioned torturer and the revolutionary bomber reverse this rule, attempting, as did the burners of heretics in the past, to destroy the opinion by destroying the person. At the same time, that other phenomenon of modern times, the psychiatric treatment of an individual for deviant opinions, represents the ultimate invasion of personality, and the final rejection of the ideal of toleration.

But what, then, of the practical activities of the opinion-holder? It has already been pointed out that actions may be limited by the need to protect the defenceless and it follows from this that even the deepest religious or moral conviction cannot be allowed to justify the infliction of pain, mutilation, or deprivation of freedom on human beings whose age, sex, or social position prevents them from defending themselves in these respects, and this limitation may well be extended to other sentient creatures who are also capable of suffering.

We may now add that opinions inextricably intermeshed with practical consequences may also be qualified by the claims of other principles of freedom—this despite the *a priori* assumption in favour of freedom that otherwise applies. While the first two cases are, as has already been pointed out, effectively covered by the protection of the defenceless principle, the third seems to raise in a distinctive way the issue of freedom of association with those whose views are offensive or deeply repugnant to others, particularly where cases arise in an educational or employment context. As Preston King wrote, with some foresight: "What would be anomalous about the sort of situation that presently concerns us is the spectacle of those who attack racialists, tribalists, religious bigots and the like being subject to legal punishment . . . while the very same people who exceed the necessary bounds of free speech go about untroubled."[16]

Precisely such a situation arose recently at a London education institution where legal sanctions and imprisonment threatened those who objected to the *presence* of a student holding racist views—a racist view here being definable as the view that some people should be adversely treated because of their race.

But the question is, should we demand institutional arrangements to spare us the compulsory company of those we abhor—those whose expressed opinions or declared political affiliation identifies them as the racialists, tribalists, and religious bigots of King's concern? In reaching a conclusion, we must bear in mind also the reply rightly given to those who demand *racial* separation in employment or education—those who promote, in other words, a racial apartheid. This is that in all such cases, if there is to be separation, it should be achieved by the objector removing himself or herself rather than by the expulsion of the person whose presence is found offensive—frequently, in both the racial and the individual case, the scapegoat on whom the sins of the community are pinned. So, paradoxical though the situation may be that King describes, it may sometimes be right to curb the activity of the protesters, and to protect the holder of unpopular or offensive opinions.

Nevertheless, it has to be recognised that employment and education provide institutional settings in which the choice of avoidance may deprive the chooser of his own education or employment. This places an obligation on those who administer such closed institutional arrangements to seek for compromise wherever possible. On the issue of principle, however, the words of Hobhouse still strike a firm and relevant note: "The Liberal does not meet opinions which he conceives to be false with toleration, as though they did not matter. He meets them with justice, and exacts for them a fair hearing."[17]

"A fair hearing" means precisely toleration of the expression of opinion, stopping short, however, of action and incitement to action at that point where the principle of protection of the defenceless must take priority. It is through this point on the toleration continuum—a continuum that stretches from opinion through the expression of opinion, to proselytizing for an opinion, to inciting to action, and finally to action itself—where the line must be drawn marking off the limits of toleration.

Notes

1. This is discussed in chap. 10.
2. H. Marcuse "Repressive Tolerance," in *A Critique of Pure Tolerance*, ed. R. P. Wolff, B. Moore, and H. Marcuse (London: Cape, 1969), p. 122-123.
3. Ibid., p. 97.
4. J. S. Mill, *On Liberty* (1859; reprint, London: Dent, 1954), p. 73.
5. *Rakovian Catechism*, preface to 1655 edition. Quoted in H. Kamen, *The Rise of Toleration* (London: Weidenfeld & Nicolson, 1967), p. 124.

6. Pierre Bayle, *Dictionnaire Historique et Critique* (1696). Quoted in Kamen, *Rise of Toleration*, p. 237.
7. James Harrington, *Oceana* (1656). Quoted in Kamen, *The Rise of Toleration*, p. 204.
8. Marcuse, "Repressive Tolerance," p. 104.
9. J. B. Bury, *History of Greece* (London: Macmillan, 1959) p. 404.
10. F. M. Cornford, (1951) *The Republic of Plato* (Oxford: Oxford University Press, 1951) p. 276.
11. Mill, *On Liberty*, p. 115.
12. Marcuse, "Repressive Toleranace," p. 115.
13. R. P. Wolff, "Beyond Tolerance," in Wolff Moore, and Marcuse, *Critique of Pure Tolerance*, p. 61.
14. P. King, *Toleration* (London: Allen & Unwin, 1976), p. 111.
15. H Arendt, "Truth and Politics," in P. Laslett, and W. G. Runciman, ed. *Philosophy, Politics and Society*, 3d ser. (Oxford: Blackwell 1978), p. 133.
16. King, *Toleration*, pp. 196–97.
17. L. T. Hobhouse, *Liberalism* (1911; reprint, New York: Oxford University Press, 1971), p. 63.

5
Return to the Cave: New Directions for Philosophy of Education

Philosophy has seen two revolutions in the present century, and philosophy of education, while certainly a follower rather than a leader in relation to the central discipline, never remains unaffected by these sea changes. The first revolution in philosophy was accomplished by the analytic tradition in its two forms: the positivism of the scientifically and mathematically oriented philosophy originating with the Vienna Circle in the 1920s and 1930s; and ordinary language philosophy stemming from Moore and represented in Britain by such figures as Austin and Wisdom. The second revolution in philosophy has been away from these logical and epistemological preoccupations under the influence of powerful pressures for philosophy to play a part in resolving the moral and political dilemmas of contemporary society. These have resulted on the whole from scientific advances that have, like the creation of Frankenstein, overtaken their authors and inventors in the areas of medicine, environment, and human relationships.

In philosophy of education, the historical position preceding the seminal reconstruction work of R. S. Peters was summed up by Archambault as "vagueness, ambiguity, pseudo-problems and pseudo-explanations, vacuous principles and impractical prescriptions."[1] The stable clearing that was necessitated by the prevalence of this approach left a stable ready for the reception of a horse of an entirely different colour. The analytic view of philosophy, which, repudiating metaphysics, restricted the function of philosophy to clarification and analysis, was paralleled by a new concept of the function of philosophy of education: to lay bare the issues; to expose the premises implicit in the reasoning of the other contributory disciplines (mainly psychology and sociology, both approached empirically); but not to determine policy. In *Ethics and Education*, Peters laid down a blueprint for the philosophy of education that largely determined the path that has been followed. The issues he identified there for philosophy of education were:

1. the analysis of educational concepts,
2. the application of ethics and social philosophy to education,
3. problems in philosophical psychology, particularly the critique of psychologists' assumptions, and
4. the examination of the logical and epistemological basis of the curriculum.[2]

The popularity of this approach followed the enthusiasm for science and scientific advance that characterized the middle years of the century. In spite of—or perhaps because of—its declared limitations, it seemed a firmer and more promising approach than the romantic progressivism associated with ill-defined theories of child development that had preceded it.

As criticism has developed of analytic philosophy, however, so some (more muted) criticism has been voiced of the parallel conception of philosophy of education. The slogan "Clarity is not enough" that was applied to philosophy proper seemed to have an even more pertinent application to philosophy of education. For education is essentially a practical pursuit.

The second revolution in philosophy, then, has resulted in practical needs being much more sympathetically viewed than was the case while the analytic approach held undisputed sway. In Plato's metaphorical story in the Republic, the philosopher who has enjoyed the clear light of contemplation of logical, ethical, and epistemological truth finds it his duty to return to the darkened underground cave where his contemporaries lie in chains debating about shadows and images. The second revolution in both philosophy and philosophy of education could be seen as a return to the cave on the part of the postanalytic school of philosophers—those who have been exposed to the tradition of clarification and the pursuit of truth in their training, but have become conscious of the need to say something to their contemporaries who are faced with ethical, social, and educational problems and see philosophy as a discipline providing answers as well as questions. While agnosticism on all issues has been a central feature of the analytic school, the possibility of neutrality has received serious challenge. Just as the economists' slogan rightly tells us that "there are no free lunches," so Marxism and the philosophy of the social sciences have convinced us that there is after all no genuinely value-free philosophy or philosophy of education. In these circumstances, philosophers have become much more willing to make a direct contribution to debate about practical policies in all the fields in which options are genuinely open to determination on ethical and philosophical grounds—in particular areas such as medicine, politics, and education.

The extent of this contrast in philosophy of education can be seen if one looks back to the narrowing of legitimate interests proposed in D. J. O'Connor's influential *An Introduction to the Philosophy of Education*.[3] There O'Connor criticises Dewey for including in *Democracy and Education* discussion of the nature and aims of education which does not fall into any conventional academic province and is essentially not philosophical. He suggests, by contrast, that apart from the task of clarification, educational theory itself should consist solely of recommendations for practice based on experimental findings in the social sciences. This view could be said to be at once too limited, and also too expansive. It is too limited in that educational innovation could consist only of improvements in techniques, but also too expansive in that it suggests a role for psychology and sociology within the classroom that these disciplines are unwilling to claim for themselves.

More recently, Glenn Langford has claimed that philosophy of education is just philosophy "with an eye to the practices and problems of those engaged in or concerned with education" and that, consequently, philosophy by itself cannot provide answers to educational problems.[4] He suggests that examination of the *language* of education will clarify the problems and reveal the sort of evidence relevant to solving them.

That philosophy of education should claim a wider role than this was seen by some as one of the vices of progressive education and something to be avoided by what Gilbert Ryle proposed as the new "methodology of education," the "Grammar of Pedagogy."[5] While some are still prepared to accept this restriction and the austere view of philosophy and philosophy of education on which it is based, philosophers of a leftist or Marxist persuasion have consciously and deliberately set out to transcend its limitations. A main tenet of their position is that the analytic view of philosophy is based on the fact-value distinction—a distinction they reject in their claim that apparent neutrality, freedom from taking up a value position, is mere self-deception. They would argue that, for example, R. S. Peters' transcendental deduction of principles of morals and education is itself value-laden and merely symptomatic of his position as a leader of the liberal educational establishment.

In looking again, then, at the function of philosophy of education and seeking a fundamental reconstruction of its outlook, certain basic questions can be identified.

1. Does the liberal-analytic approach itself embody concealed substantive values?
2. If it does, does this represent a denial of the fact-value distinction?
3. Does liberalism actually involve neutrality, or is it better defined in terms of commitment to a range of values, some of them directly relevant to specific problems in the field of education?

It is in terms of the answers to these questions that I would see the outline of a new approach to the philosophy of education, one that takes as its starting point the advances recently made through the application of a liberal, humanistic, and analytic approach, but does not remain imprisoned within the confines of analysis alone. In Hegelian terms, if the analytic position is seen as thesis, the radical criticism to which that position has been subjected can be seen as antithesis and a form of positive liberalism can be evolved from the two to form a valid and useful synthesis.

Substantive Values and the Analytic Tradition

Particularly in the case of political and moral education, philosophers writing within the analytic tradition have tended to draw a distinction between two levels of principles: those that are formal—providing the logical framework for the kind of discourse in question—and those that are substantive, open to legitimate questioning and essentially a matter of choice or allegiance. As far as a general framework for education is concerned, a parallel distinction can be drawn between principles (for example, fairness or respect for persons) and particular educational practices, such as integration, mixed ability teaching, problem and subject-centred approaches.

The underlying assumption of these distinctions is that in each case the first half of the contrast represents something which can be characterised as essential but value-free, while the second half of the contrast, though admittedly involving value judgements, is conceived of as offering a range of choices, any of which may be compatible with a liberal position. The alternatives listed are seen as genuine alternatives and commitment to any of them as genuinely open to choice. What is not seen as open to choice, however, is the commitment implied in the first half of the contrast—to impartiality, to an honest and open approach to argument, to truth, to treating other persons as persons. In an article written in 1976, Robin Haack argued that this so-called formal position is in fact not formal, logical, or uncommitted at all.[6] Indeed it is arguable that the evaluative nature of the principles listed can be recognised simply by consideration of what they involve. This includes, in particular, recognition of the natural authority of rationality—a value which is fundamental to the Western cultural tradition, in contrast to other traditions either more concrete or more mystical in their nature, as well as to the sophisticated conception of philosophy represented by the analytic tradition.

Rationality itself, as Peters argued, involves the principle of impartiality, which, in turn, involves the rejection of arbitrariness and an indifference to the authorship of an opinion as a factor in judging it. Again, this is more readily recognised as a substantive moral position by contrasting it with the claims of those prepared to defend a partisan approach. For example, Trotsky in a more specifically ethical context attacked the liberal emphasis on impartiality of moral judgement and defended a partisan or nonimpartial approach in these terms: "A slave-holder who through cunning and violence shackles a slave in chains, and a slave who through cunning and violence breaks the chains—let not the contemptible eunuchs tell us that they are equals before a court of morality!"[7]

In terms of liberal morality, double standards such as these can only be justified if relevant differences are cited; and the particular example chosen by Trotsky weakens his argument just because where slaves and slave-owners are concerned, relevant differences are in fact involved. What is inconsistent with liberal ethics, though, is a *truly* partisan approach. It is in this respect that liberal ethics can be seen as a facet of a liberal approach to truth and enquiry rather than—as it has been represented—a set of necessary presuppositions of practical discourse. The openness to argument, the demand for impartiality, the condemnation of double standards, the rejection of authority and dogma that the approach epitomises, are all, as Marxist and other critics have maintained, substantive values. Peters' transcendental principles do, it must be admitted, embody a moral stance no less than the range of alternative practical positions that can be derived from them.

Returning to the examples of morals and politics mentioned to begin with, in the debate about moral education it is possible to argue that there are similarly not two levels of principles, one formal and secure, the other substantive and open to argument, but simply moral principles of a more general or more specific form. And where politics is concerned, a liberal political position does not, as is sometimes thought, require agreement on a noncontroversial framework for political choice, with substantive decision making at another level. In all these cases, whether the object is truth, moral right, political justice, or educational good, substantive values are involved even at the most abstract and general level.

The charge, then, that the currently dominant position in philosophy of education—the one that derives from the analytic approach in mainstream philosophy—is not value-free, but, instead, embodies substantive values, must, after all, be conceded. The principles on which the analytic approach is based do indeed represent a moral stance and one in keeping with a broadly liberal ethical and political position. It remains to consider, though, whether this is, in fact, the criticism it appears to be, or whether, on the contrary, it may be accepted as an illuminating comment on the situation.

The Admission of Value and the Fact-Value Distinction

One reason why the admission that latent values lie concealed within an approach which claims to confine itself to the elucidation of facts and their logical implications seems damaging is that this appears to violate a basic principle of that approach: the separation of facts and values. Antony Flew has remarked that the fact-value distinction has become old-fashioned without ever being disproved, and this suggests that the question, "Is the fact-value distinction being violated?" poses the prior question, "Is the fact-value distinction valid?"[8]

But first it is worth making clear just what is the point of this distinction. Essentially two stages of argument are involved. The first stage of the argument simply sets on one side the world of empirical facts—facts which may be recognised or observed by one or more of the physical senses. On the other side, it places the world of moral judgement, whether this is interpreted in psychological terms or as in some sense or other objective and accessible to a moral sense, intuition, or conscience. Following from recognition of the different status of these two areas, the second stage of the argument draws attention to Hume's famous argument that an "ought" cannot be derived from an "is" and asserts that any deduction of values from facts must be invalid.[9]

Nevertheless, it can scarcely be argued that facts are totally irrelevant to values, and a number of philosophers have recently been prepared to argue for the deducibility that Hume apparently denied ("apparently" because MacIntyre has pointed out that Hume might conceivably be interpreted as saying that the derivation is very *difficult* rather than impossible.[10] Philippa Foot, for instance, has argued that certain kinds of facts can be seen as plainly irrelevant to moral judgement. She cites as an example the case of someone who claims to attach moral significance to the idea of looking at hedgehogs by the light of the moon.[11] More seriously, Mary Midgley has argued that facts about human nature and the kind of physical and emotional satisfaction or suffering to which it is prone are importantly relevant to the making of moral judgements.[12] And John Searle has presented a technical argument to support the idea that certain kinds of fact, for example, that a person has made a promise, do logically entail certain obligations—in this case to attempt, other things being equal, to carry out the promise.[13]

None of these arguments, however, show that the first stage of the fact-value distinction is invalid, and as far as their criticisms appear to apply to the second stage of the argument, they depend upon obscuring the line between deducibility and relevance. Searle, it is true, is arguing for a straight logical derivation, but the case of promising is a special one in which a certain performance (saying "I promise") itself constitutes a kind of moral commitment; at the same time, use of the term *promising* without quotation marks or italics by an observer or commentator implies the speaker's acceptance of this convention.

In general, though, it is undeniable that our moral judgements about the world are framed in relation to what is done, what happens, what goes on—in other words, to empirical facts. In this sense, the world of facts is certainly relevant to the world of value—indeed, it is its point and purpose. But the distinction between the two worlds is still one it is important to maintain. Otherwise two undesirable consequences follow: First, mention of facts will be thought to be decisive in concluding a moral argument; and second, there will be a risk that people will lose sight of the truth that there is very often a choice in human affairs about what to do. In personal life, decisions have to be framed in the light of ideals as well as of facts—something that applies to decisions in education, too. It is more to the point to see values as deriving from ideals rather than from existing facts since future facts are open to determination by the choices people make in the present and have made in the past.

There can be no objection then, to accepting that both in mainstream analytic philosophy and in the philosophy of education that it has engendered, a commitment to certain ideals and values has indeed underlain all discussions, even those of a most apparently narrow logical and analytic nature. (It might be necessary to except from this generalisation the kind of empty expansion of tautologies that is the province of formal logic, although even here commitment to rational and open enquiry is presupposed). In this sense, then, the charge that facts and values are not being kept apart is well made. But that there is a direct relation of entailment between facts and values that preempts all choice—the assumption that is really the point at issue for defenders of the fact-value distinction—remains without foundation and quite unaffected by arguments designed to show that those who argue for it are themselves committed to a particular moral stance. Just as choice without freedom is a contradiction in terms, so a belief in the total determination of values by facts would make morality impossible. Recognition of the relevance of facts to values, then, cannot and need not be taken to the point of deducibility. The consequence of admitting the value basis of analytic philosophy is not, after all, denial of the fact-value distinction. And an analytic philosophy of education is not shown to be violating this distinction when its moral foundations are laid bare.

The Liberal-Analytic Tradition and Neutrality

The sense in which the discovery of substantive values underlying the analytic approach within philosophy of education can be taken as an exposé of a deficiency in that approach can now be seen to be extremely limited. To present an evaluation as a logical truth may be confused and is certainly confusing, but the strength of the position involved is not necessarily undermined by greater clarity as to what that position actually is. Indeed, considerable advantage is to be gained from a conscious shift within a liberal-empiricist approach to philosophy of education from the unattainable ideal of neutrality to a more conscious commitment to values and ideals. That only Marxists should appear to have a defined position on substantive moral matters—and this while repudiating objective morality altogether—is an unfortunate consequence of the excessive austerity and deliberate avoidance of moral commitment that has characterised the analytic tradition until recently.

Admittedly, there may be a price to be paid for conscious commitment to particular values. This is the risk of making a contribution that is ephemeral rather than permanent—one that follows too closely the popular trends of the day. But it is worth taking this risk in order to become responsive to the issues exercising those who must make practical decisions as to what to do within defined time limits and in particular circumstances.

If a liberal-analytic philosophy of education, then, is not value-free, what are the substantive values to which it is committed? One range of values has already been mentioned. These are the ones that follow from the commitment to impartiality, and since they involve openness to argument, they lead directly to the central liberal value of toleration. Indeed, the values of liberalism as a political and social ideal have, via their ethical dimension, analogues in the area of enquiry and the pursuit of truth (one way of characterising philosophy). So allied to the commitment to toleration there emerges an emphasis on individualism and on the pluralism that results from permitting the operation of individual judgement, criticism, and autonomy. These values were already present, however, in the phrase "respect for persons" which is usually linked with impartiality as a basic presumption of the analytic approach in philosophy of education.

If we seek to specify the pressing practical issues for our day outside a purely educational context, these emerge as issues to which both these identifiable values—individualism and toleration—are fundamental. They are issues concerned with race, with the position of women, with the distribution of resources between rich and poor; with the impact of technology on people; with war and peace; with the planet as a support system for human beings. While these are issues much wider than education, education can no more be neutral about them than can, or ought to be, philosophy. They remain, however, matters of controversy and so, in considering how education can best relate to them, questions of the control of education and the content of the curriculum inevitably arise. Approaches to these fundamental issues are differently defined by different members of a particular society. In coming to terms with this problem, it becomes necessary to ask and to answer the question: are the ends of education primarily political and social or primarily personal and cultural? These are questions with which a socially aware philosophy of education must be concerned.

But once the questions are raised, it is clear that the liberal answer to them is bound to be different from that of a political dogmatist whether of the Left or the Right. The dominant goal of autonomy of judgement means that a liberal perspective will be opposed to state control of education in any form that might permit the state—centralised government—to monopolise the formation of opinion on these or any issues, or to compel conformity. Its concern will always be that of openness and it will wish to promote this value even at the expense of such desirable alternatives as equality, happiness, or fraternity.

Where it contributes discussion of a concrete issue like race or sex discrimination, its conclusions will be shaped by recognition of a principle of equality of respect. It may conclude that policies like positive discrimination actually violate this principle; but without contradiction it may also decide that means must be found to avoid early and subtle forms of indoctrination in attitudes that may be characterised as sexist or racist. Questions of the distribution of resources, on the other hand, or of technological innovation, of international relations, or of war and peace are of indirect rather than direct concern for philosophy of education. For while these issues need to be given the importance in education that they deserve, they are in the end problems to be solved by those who are being educated rather than by the educators. Those who are being educated need to be presented, therefore, with the questions rather than the answers and equipped with the kind of problem-solving tools that are relevant to this type of question. These will include clarity of vision, honesty of approach, and a good deal of hard practical knowledge and understanding. The exact role of education in relation to these issues—how to educate but not to indoctrinate—is something that a more practically oriented philosophy of education can profitably investigate.

Finally, one further consequence of recognising the values implicit in a liberal approach to education is that its commitment to pluralism becomes explicit. As a consequence, it is easier to see that a plural society must be committed to the cultivation of a variety of talent. It cannot be the role of an educational system which is committed to liberal values to impose homogeneity and uniformity. Hence, some provision for identifying special talent, some deliberate cultivation of elites in differing fields must be preferred to any policy of levelling out, where this means levelling down. Thus it becomes clear that the fostering of diversity of talent implies a liberal education in the more usual sense of this term. A liberal education in the traditional sense is a prerequisite of a liberal society, since if various talents are to be recognised and cultivated, then no main area of human thought or activity may be omitted, at least at an early stage, from the curriculum, although later specialisation will be both possible and necessary.

In conclusion, then, it is possible to say that certain values are indeed implicit in the recent analytic interpretation of philosophy of education, and these do have real implications for educational practice. And once a liberal-analytic approach to philosophy of education is recognised as an aspect of political and moral liberalism, it is easier to see why neutrality on practical issues is neither necessary nor desirable. In particular, it becomes clear that such an approach has implications for the organisation of education, in that its answers to questions about control are biased toward individual choices rather than toward centralised bureaucracy. And it has implications about the form and content of education within whatever organisational framework is adopted. It is not, nor should it be, blind, deaf, and dumb where the issues of the day are concerned. It is against discrimination and for the secure and balanced economic and political conditions which favour cultural development. It must give priority, however, to individual autonomy and judgement and, in confronting the outstanding problems of the age, defer to that judgement, not ossifying any one solution but ready for perpetual revision of solutions in the light of new argument and new development. But subject to this crucial qualification, the right direction for both philosophy and philosophy of education today involves a much more direct concern for these practical problems and an end to the obsessive navel-gazing that certain kinds of philosophical analysis suggest to the outside world.

Notes

Reprinted from *Educational Analysis* 4 (1982): 93–101, by permission of the editor and publishers.

1. R. D. Archambault, ed., *Philosophical Analysis and Education* (London: Routledge & Kegan Paul, 1965), p. 8.
2. R. S. Peters, *Ethics and Education* (London: Allen & Unwin, 1966), pp. 18–19.
3. D. J. O'Connor, *Introduction to Philosophy of Education* (London: Routledge & Kegan Paul, 1957).
4. G. Langford, *Philosophy and Education* (London: Macmillan, 1968), p. 14.
5. G. Ryle, *The Concept of Mind* (London: Hutchinson, 1949), p. 318.
6. Robin Haack, "Philosophies of Education," *Philosophy* 51 (1976): 159–76.
7. L. Trotsky, *Their Morals and Ours* (New York: Pathfinder Press, 1975).
8. A. Flew, "On Not Deriving 'Ought' from 'Is,'" in *The Is/Ought Question*, ed. W. D. Hudson, (London: Macmillan, 1969), p. 135.
9. Quoted in full, pp. 3–4.
10. A. MacIntyre, "Hume on 'Is' and 'Ought,' *Philosophical Review* 68 (1959): 451–68.
11. P. Foot, "Moral Arguments," *Mind* 67 (1958): 502–13.
12. M. Midgley, *Beast and Man* (Ithaca, N.Y.: Cornell University Press, 1978), chap. 9.
13. J. R. Searle, "How to Derive 'Ought' from 'Is,' *Philosophical Review* 73 (1964): 43–58.

6
Ethical Objectivity and Moral Education

The ethical analysis a person accepts makes all the difference to the policy that person is prepared to recommend for moral education. For instance, outside religious circles the prevailing viewpoint today is essentially subjectivist—hence the popularity of approaches to moral education which stress autonomy, leaving the individual ultimately to form his own ethical opinions, though possibly on some broad agreed procedural basis. The only policy open to an objectivist, on the other hand, and hence the policy most favoured by those whose ethical basis is religious, is that of securing conformity to society's values.

This position, or something like it, would probably be widely accepted. But I would like to suggest that not only is it wrong to draw any such direct inferences as these between ethical theory and moral education, but that there could be equally sound justification for drawing precisely opposite conclusions. In other words, instead of linking subjectivism and autonomy, objectivism and conformity, as valid a case can be made out for linking objectivism with autonomy and subjectivism with conformity to society's values.

I take the subjectivist view in ethics to be one that emphasises the fundamental role of personal choice in moral evaluation and decision, though it may involve a descriptive concept of morality as well, in terms of the values actually dominant in a society. This is the sociological or anthropological use of the term—the standpoint of the external observer. The objectivist position I take to be one that assigns a place to rational argument and to the notions of correctness and incorrectness in moral evaluation. The objectivist will probably think in terms of conscience or a moral sense that he will ascribe to human beings on a wider basis than that of a particular society or social group. It could be said that both concepts of morality have a part to play in human affairs, that there is both a morality of localised social convention, and also a deeper level of universal morality: the Greeks' "natural law," modern "human rights." But I would suggest that it is not necessary to settle these questions in order to engage in moral education, and, in particular, I would attack the standard assumption that subjectivism must be associated with an open approach to moral education, and objectivism with a closed and dogmatic approach.

To clarify what is at issue here, the advocate of neutrality may be regarded as holding the view that it is not the function of a moral educator to be partisan as regards any particular moral viewpoint; if he is to avoid the undesirable stigma of indoctrinating, he must simply give his pupils factual information about (a) the empirical world, and (b) the formal rules governing moral discourse, thus placing them in a position to reach their own conclusions on moral matters. Bertrand Russell once gave expression to a viewpoint like this when he condemned the prescribing of definite opinions on politics, morals, and religion—the teaching of some one orthodoxy—claiming that this excludes from the teaching profession men who combine honesty with intellectual vigour.

> When a school accepts as part of its task the teaching of an opinion which cannot be intellectually defended (as practically all schools do), it is compelled to give the impression that those who hold an opposite opinion are wicked, since otherwise it cannot generate the passion required for repelling the assaults of reason. Thus for the sake of orthodoxy the children are rendered uncharitable, intolerant, cruel and bellicose. This is unavoidable so long as definite opinions are prescribed on politics, morals and religion.[1]

The implication behind these remarks is that moral values are to be chosen rather than discovered—that morality is an area of uncertainty and preference rather than of certainty and closed obligations; but it is important to notice the tacit reference to another and assumed value system—that to be uncharitable, intolerant, cruel, and bellicose is wrong.

It is not surprising that such ambiguities should creep in, for it is, in fact, more difficult than it might appear to adopt consistent moral tolerance. Most people do, in fact, wish and need to participate in as well as to comment upon the moral scene, and this is particularly true of those whose business is the upbringing of children. Hence the frequently observed phenomenon of moral language seeping back in disguised form into the vocabulary of those who wish to avoid it: for example, *antisocial* or *counterproductive*—terms which transparently serve only to substitute for the simple but rejected *wrong*.

Various authors, though, have more recently endorsed the notion of the uncertainty of specific morality and have allowed this to shape their approach to moral education. John Wilson once referred to the "uncertainty" of the moral area as a reason for avoiding specific instruction on substantive matters of morals, defining *uncertain* as "not true that any sane and sensible person, when presented with the relevant facts and arguments, would necessarily hold the beliefs."[2] A lack of publicly accepted evidence for such beliefs made instruction in moral matters, in his view, indoctrination rather than education. It was from this early starting point that he embarked on his later more extensive work in this field. Although his more recent work includes very much more positive and specific recommendations for moral education, his earlier position was influential in separating specific practical guidance from the task of the inculcation of moral capacities.[3] R. F. Atkinson, too, argued that "there can be moral teaching, instruction in, as opposed to instruction about, morality, only if there are criteria of truth, cogency, correctness in the field."[4] Conversely, in a paper called "Moral Authority and Moral Education," Grenville Wall opposes the policy of neutrality as regards practical moral issues, on the ground that there is in fact an area of objective moral knowledge in which it is possible to be expert, or, as he prefers to say, an authority.[5]

If these views were correct, then the prospects for moral education would be discouraging in the extreme; for it would mean that it would be necessary to settle the more fundamental question of the ultimate basis of ethics before being able to embark on any such programme. Fortunately, a little careful reflection suggests that it is, in fact, unnecessary to embark on such an extensive preliminary venture, for a subjectivist, or even an emotivist, although he will give a different account of it, may have an equally strong desire to influence, particularly his *own* children, in the direction of sharing his moral attitudes—shunning cruelty, for instance, or avoiding prejudice. This will be closer, however, to the way in which he may wish them to share his own tastes—in music, perhaps, or literature—rather than to the way in which he approaches their education in matters of fact. It is, in other words, not necessary to be an ethical objectivist in order to be against the concept of a neutral moral educator. Moreover, even if it could be established that there *is* objective moral knowledge, this would not in itself rule out a policy of moral neutrality, since, as in other areas of the curriculum, a programme of "finding out" might be preferred to one of "being told." What is being suggested here is that the question of the objectivity or otherwise of ethics, and the question of moral education, are logically independent.

With regard to the objectivity of ethics, it is necessary to make comparisons with other areas of the curriculum in order to see whether there is the kind of radical contrast that is assumed. If such a comparison is made, it is clear that very little possesses the type of certainty in terms of which the contrast is framed, and, in particular, philosophical discussion of the foundations of science and of mathematics—those paradigms of certainty in the classroom—demonstrate this most effectively. Moreover, even within the context of assumptions about scientific and mathematical certainty, problems can arise, such as, for example, disagreement concerning the teaching of Darwinian evolutionary theory or the abuse of mathematics for indoctrinatory purposes. A lack of publicly accepted standards, then, is a charge which may or may not be accepted by the ethical objectivist (who does not have to believe that everyone must share his insights) but, in any case, does not clearly separate out the area of morals from everything else with which it is proposed to acquaint children.

This argument, which attempts to link objectivism in ethics with dogmatic or conformist goals in moral education, is the converse of the one already mentioned that assumes a link between subjectivism in ethics and a policy of neutrality—essentially mediated by a presumption of agnosticism or indifference with regard to substantive moral matters. This argument, although it appears most strikingly at the level of children and moral education, has a general application at the level of moral relations between equals. The proposition widely put forward, but nevertheless fallacious, is that subjectivism (or, sometimes, liberalism) entails that no moral judgement is any more "right" than any other; that one's moral judgements apply only to oneself; and hence that there can be no case for proselytizing. For example, I may not believe in war; but I will not hold that nonpacifists are wrong when they fight. To put the point differently: subjectivism seems to entail that I judge only for myself and cannot judge for others. In a very fundamental sense, it seems to entail moral neutrality as regards other people's obligations—only if I know what they think they ought to do, can I say what in fact they ought to do.

But this view is essentially incoherent.[6] It entails the abdication of all moral censure, praise, blame, and evaluation. Its incoherence lies in the fact that the remaining use of "right" that is left after the application to other people has been removed has, because it is entirely particular and individualistic, been drained of all meaning. "I ought to do x," according to this interpretation of subjectivism, becomes indistinguishable from "I am going to do x." It follows that I must be able to make judgements about what other people ought to do if I am to be able to make judgements about what I myself should do.

It is nevertheless undeniable that other people's ideas of right and wrong will differ in significant respects from my own. If there cannot be unanimity, then, what must be concluded about the differing moral concepts that exist within a given society, and even more in different societies? What should *not* be concluded is that all are equally right or wrong, for this would itself be another moral judgement, and one it is virtually impossible to make with consistency. For in committing myself to any moral view on any issue, I deny it. The mere making of such a judgement suggests that it is made from outside the human framework, by an external observer who is not himself a part of the world of which he judges that all views are equal. But, of course, no one can possess this detachment, for everyone is involved in the world of human action as participants as well as spectators. Insofar as they can make an effort to believe that they can, and that ethical subjectivism entails that they should, hold such a position, the position they are committed to is less one of moral neutrality than of moral inertia and indecision. Commitment to any moral viewpoint inevitably makes one into a proselytizer, and into a judge of one's fellow men.

It follows, then, that just as objectivism is not necessarily linked with dogmatism, so subjectivism is not essentially connected to neutrality. Paradoxically, too, the subjectivist may have less reason to respect the conscience, and hence the autonomy, of the individual than has the objectivist. For the objectivist will be concerned to stress the importance of moral concepts, but must recognise the fallibility of human beings in judging objective facts; so that alternative viewpoints will merit serious consideration and their expression will be protected. But the subjectivist, on the other hand, cannot attach meaning to this generous concession of the possibility of error, and, moreover, may regard moral matters as trivial and unimportant.

It is clear, then, that as a basis for formulating a policy for moral education objectivism and subjectivism do not, after all, provide clear guidelines. The degree of commitment of the subjectivist on the one hand and the willingness of the objectivist to recognise the possibility of error on the other must critically affect their position on the openness of any moral education programme.

It is questionable, then, whether the contemporary preference for subjectivist accounts of ethics need, after all, entail the view that an educator should be morally neutral, and should not adopt substantive moral positions in relation to specific issues. However, in "Moral Autonomy and the Liberal Theory of Moral Education," Wall offered a definition of a liberal theory of moral education, linking it to the notion of autonomy as a favoured liberal aim:

> If moral indoctrination is thought of as the attempt to implant a specific set of moral beliefs, then it seems that moral education must be open-ended and non-doctrinal if children are to emerge growing in autonomy. At the end, if not throughout the course of their moral education, children must be allowed to make up their own minds about moral issues. Moral education must concentrate on the teaching of the procedures of moral reasoning rather than on any specific content.[7]

This, Wall claimed, was his conception of what a liberal theory of moral education involved, and it has already been suggested that such a policy is indeed the recommendation of a number of writers approaching this subject from a philosophical point of view. Something, therefore, must now be said about the details of this approach, a common factor of which is the drawing of a distinction between a level at which commitment is assumed, and a level at which agnosticism or at least autonomy is appropriate.

These two levels are sometimes associated with two levels of principles—first-order and second-order principles. An example of a first-order principle would be "people ought not to tell lies," while an example of a second-order principle would be a principle of impartiality or fairness. In this case, it is likely to be argued that direct inculcation of the first type of principle should be replaced by the development and encouragement of specific moral abilities. R. S. Peters gives a special place to what may be called second-order principles, and in his view, these include, as well as impartiality, consideration or respect for persons. A good example of the way such a distinction works in practice comes to the fore in connection with the debate on sex education. Here it may be argued that the function of sex education may be to seek to instill commitment to an ideal such as that of respect for persons (not treating another person simply as a means for one's personal gratification), but that any practical inference from this must be left to the person concerned. It could not, in other words, be appropriate for the sex educator to recommend either chastity or promiscuity. This distinction is described by Wall as a distinction between the *form* and the *content* of morality—the view that one should teach people *how* rather than *what* to think—and as essentially marking the borderline between indoctrination and education.

Although this is the intention underlying this distinction, it seems that the difficulty of justifying such a distinction has been underestimated. Here the experience of liberal devisers of collections of teaching materials on such issues as race or sex are significant. What is being sought, essentially, is a compromise between holding and propounding doctrinaire, fixed principles to be adhered to whatever the circumstances, and a wholly situational ethic within which no constants would apply.

However, although there may be principles of a greater or lesser degree of generality, and there may well be a case for preferring the more general to the more specific, it is a mistake to suppose that there could be any *logical* difference between principles, such as is needed to make the two-level theory succeed. The one exception here is the universalizability principle, but of this I would say only that if universalizability is indeed a *logical* property of moral discourse, then it cannot itself be a moral principle of a special and superior sort. Part of the plausibility of the two-level theory does seem to arise from fusing these two concepts of universalizability—the logical and the normative—into the notion of fairness or justice, or indeed even of respect for persons.

Once the possibility of compromise is dismissed, the idea that liberal moral education might involve at any level complete openness, agnosticism, or lack of commitment becomes less plausible. For it must be admitted that liberalism *does* involve commitment to *some* principles. It is essentially a moral point of view, entailing particular policies for action in the political, social, and interpersonal spheres.

A coherent case for a policy of neutrality has been made out neither by those who make a distinction between first- and second-order principles, nor by those who, as a matter of ethical analysis, reject the objectivity of morals. Among the former group are those, like Stenhouse, whose espousal of a neutralist approach is presented as a matter of strategy only—they are in no doubt that, for example, racism is wrong, but consider that directly telling children that racism is wrong is not the best way to achieve the agreed outcome: the rejection of racialism. Whether one agrees with these approaches will depend, then, if one shares this point of view, on how far as a matter of empirical fact this policy can be seen to work in practice.

The concern here, however, is not with this factual dispute, but with the position of those who fall into the second category, and whose neutralist recommendations are based on a genuine uncertainty on matters of ethics. Again, a further distinction can be made between uncertainty concerning a substantial ethical issue—something that genuinely bedevils the discussion on sex education and marks it out as a very different area from that of race relations—and uncertainty as a matter of principle. It is this latter position that is mistakenly adopted by those who, having considered alternative accounts of the basis of ethics, are unable to accept the thesis of objectivism and believe that this places ethical and moral certainty beyond the reach of the educator.

It must be stressed, however, that this does not mean the replacement of the goal of autonomy with that of conformity to the values of society in any sociologically observed sense. While talk of autonomy might well be dropped because of the misleading interpretations to which it has proved subject, the goal of conformity cannot but be adopted by people who attempt to influence others in moral matters; but it is the goal of conformity to their own ideals which follows as a logical consequence of understanding what it is to have ideals. It follows then, that there are as many moral education policies as there are moral educators. Such an anarchic conclusion, however, may well be harmless. For it may be, after all, that a fortunate concurrence of opinion within a liberal society as to values will avoid the widely diverging practices that might otherwise follow, and will produce an approximate unanimity of practice that consideration of the theoretic foundations of ethics is unable to supply.

Notes

This chapter is a longer version of a paper originally delivered at the World Congress of Education on Values and the School, held at the University of Quebec in Trois-Rivières, Canada, in July 1981 and was originally published in *Journal of Moral Education* 13 (1983): 131–36; reprinted by permission of the editor and publishers.

1. B. Russell, *Sceptical Essays*, (London: Allen & Unwin, 1977), pp. 198–200.
2. J. Wilson, "Education and Indoctrination," in *Aims in Education*, ed. T. H. B. Hollins (Manchester: Manchester University Press, 1964), pp. 27–28.
3. See particularly, J. Wilson, N. Williams, and B. Sugarman, *An Introduction to Moral Education* (Harmondsworth: Penguin, 1967).
4. R. F. Atkinson, "*Instruction and Indoctrination*," in R. D. Archambault *Philosophical Analysis and Education*, ed. (London: Routledge & Kegan Paul, 1967), p. 176.
5. G. Wall, "Moral Authority and Moral Education," *Journal of Moral Education* 4, no. 2 (February 1975): 95–99.
6. This argument is developed at more length in chap. 10, pp. 125–134.
7. G. Wall, "Moral Autonomy and the Liberal Theory of Moral Education," *Journal of Philosophy of Education*, formerly, *Proceedings of the Philosophy of Education Society* 8 (1974): 222–36.

7
Education and Contemporary Issues: The Problem of Political Relevance

To what extent should education be socially relevant? If to any extent at all, what form should this social relevance take? Should educators stand aside from contentious contemporary issues, or should it be considered a task for the teaching profession to identify the important moral, social, and political issues of the day and then to approach them consciously and openly in the framework of the school curriculum? Is education to be seen as a reforming or a conserving force, as the midwife of the new society or as the guardian of culture and tradition? And to what extent should schools and the education system itself be used or transformed to serve political and social ends?

These questions reflect current concern with the political dimensions of education. For liberal social traditions have made those who live in the later years of the twentieth century acutely sensitive to the need to limit political power, and to resist invasions of personal liberty and privacy in the many spheres where an increasingly mechanised and bureaucratised state apparatus shows a tendency to creeping control. Of these areas, education must be considered the most important, partly because of the many years each member of a modern industrialised society spends within the education system, and partly because these encroachments on individual personality, if such they are, begin at an age and stage when the individual is unable to be critically aware of his or her own situation. So slogans about keeping education out of politics, and politics out of education, must have an initial appeal to those whose values are broadly liberal. On the other hand, the charge that education is politically and socially irrelevant may be thought damning from the viewpoint of liberalism itself. An education that is cut loose from the dominating concerns of the moment, or an education system that is indifferent to social needs, is not necessarily to be commended. The question, then, is whether some reconciliation of these two positions is possible. Can relevance to the crucial issues of the day be achieved without making education itself political?

But before any discussion of this question can be attempted, it has to be recognised that the assumption that a political conception of education is a bad thing will not pass unchallenged and D. Hargreaves, a writer who considers the social and political nature of education to be both important and undeniable, writes of his own "passionate belief that educational reform can improve social justice and national efficiency."[1] However, he also comments: "Education has little to contribute directly to a more just distribution of wealth; the most we can hope is that, with appropriate legislation . . . we can reduce the extent to which the educational system actually contributes to the maintenance of economic and occupational inequalities."[2]

This position may be contrasted with a more moderate claim that education can play a part in alerting students to the major political and social questions of the day. Hargreaves's position implies the stronger thesis that these problems and their solution have already been identified, and that the education system can be used as a form of social engineering to contribute to their solution. This interpretation is confirmed when he adds:

> Education cannot directly and of itself produce an end to inequalities. But an acceptance of that proposition does not entail a denial that education could exercise an important and unique role in social amelioration. With legislative support, and in concert with direct political and economic reforms, the education system could make that contribution. To that end we must refuse to confine secondary education to the culture of individualism and design a secondary education with more self-conscious social and political objectives. Otherwise the school will continue to act as a conservative force, reflecting and confirming the status quo rather than generating the will and the skill through which we can make a better society.[3]

Hargreaves later goes on to write of the fraud involved in hiding behind an apolitical mask, saying: "By depoliticising their work, the teachers make their task more, not less, difficult for they are thus prevented from developing an explicit philosophy of the relation between education and society."[4]

Other writers, too, have pressed the need for teachers to be consciously and overtly political. Pateman, for example, writes: "The obligation to be biased falls on teachers, I think, because their work situation gives them greater freedom to do and say what they want. . . . If things were other than they are, the attempt to be neutral and unbiased in the classroom, whether doomed to failure or not, might well be justified. As it is, the attempt is not only bound to fail but to turn into its opposite, discouraging rather than promoting independent thought."[5] Here Pateman echoes the view expressed by Marcuse in "Repressive Tolerance" that the only option is one form or another of bias. In the end it will be necessary to return to this problem of the teacher's role and attitude, teacher neutrality or teacher bias and commitment. But initially the implications of attempting to transform the educational system itself for social purposes deserve serious consideration.

First, though, it must be admitted that there is nothing unusual in seeking to use education in this way. The use of the education system to achieve social justice has virtually always been a goal of educational reformers, while social planners have also seen education as an important tool for their task. The ideas of Plato and Dewey both provide examples of philosophies of education that are linked closely to particular social and political ideals. The education of the Guardians was an essential aspect of Plato's Republic, while Dewey regarded the democratisation of education—the introduction of learner-oriented, cooperative and practical approaches—as essential to the democratisation of society. By this, Dewey meant the shift from a class-based, work-differentiated society to one based on equal respect and shared endeavours.

While philosophers have applied their social ideals to educational policies, the observation that practical-minded social planners are equally convinced of the potential of education to effect social transformation is confirmed by the fact that educational reform regularly follows the upheavals of war, when the need to restructure society itself is felt acutely and keenly. Apart from such moments of trauma and crisis, though, the need to make education responsive to the perceived needs of society is something widely assumed by politicians and the people they represent. If, for example, numeracy and literacy are considered vital for the functioning of society, then there will be pressure to see that these capacities are seriously cultivated. If, on the other hand, it is thought that the pocket calculator, the cassette, and the personal computer can replace these skills, then there will be pressure to replace work on the development of numeracy and literacy with work judged to be more socially rewarding and important. Again, if scientific advance is seen as vital for the survival of society, then schools will be urged to promote scientific and technological education. It must be admitted, then, that at least one highly influential approach to education takes as its basis responsiveness to social need.

Where this is so, then there is a sense in which decisions about education cannot but be political. And parallel to the pressure from writers like Hargreaves to pursue equality through the transformation of the education system, there may be pressure from other directions to pursue goals like social order and cohesiveness. For example, commenting on race riots in Britain, Geoffrey Partington offers a formula by which reforms in the education system could lead to the elimination of street disorders, specifying that "the schools, like the streets, must be bastions of law and order."[6] And while Hargreaves, to attain his end, recommends the introduction of a core curriculum and integrated studies in a comprehensive or all-ability school setting in preference to an individualist and competitive school system based on a secular version of the Protestant ethic, others, such the authors of the Black Papers, published as comment on the British educational system, recommend a differentiated and highly specialised education which rewards effort and skill as a preparation for a meritocratically organised society.

There is, then, a political conception of the school system, and different political ideals will be reflected in different educational structures and policies. It follows that an educational system may be said to be politically and socially relevant simply because it is used to achieve ends that are essentially political. But the aim of making education responsive to social needs must be distinguished from that of using it to achieve social ends. And manipulation of society through manipulation of the education system is not the only way to secure a politically and socially relevant education. For where the aim of social reconstruction takes precedence over more distinctively educational objectives, this involves a notion of education that is essentially secondary and derivative. In other words, whatever socially useful ends education can be made to serve, its primary purpose remains internal to it.

While this point may be obscured at the earlier stages of education, it is very clearly demonstrated at the level of higher education. Here, too immediate and uncritical a response to pressures that are economic, political, or narrowly utilitarian can clearly be seen to result in policies being accepted by universities that conflict with the very point and purpose of their existence. A university, for example, which accepts the kind of productivity goals that would commend themselves to commercial enterprises, calculating the contributions of its members in terms of research grants and the capacity of subjects of study to attract commercial funding, has abandoned its role as the repository of those nonutilitarian and noncommercial pursuits and concerns that are in a more fundamental sense the essence of university education.

This concept of education as a self-justifying enterprise, which has been particularly associated with the work and contribution of R. S. Peters, is the hallmark of a liberal and humanistic concept of education. It involves the rejection of overt instrumentalism as applied to the education system, and its horizons are wider than the purely immediate and parochial. It takes seriously the notion of a cultural heritage, but it interprets this concept on the broadest possible basis. But if this is the conception of education to be preferred, the question is whether it can avoid the charge of practical remoteness that is so often laid against it. Are there, in particular, ways in which education, without being used for purposes alien to itself, may nevertheless contribute to the solution of our current dilemmas?

It is important for a liberal conception of education to connect with these issues, for if it ever was the case that scholarship might responsibly be pursued away from the concerns of the world, the present day is one that leaves no safe retreat for those who simply wish to continue teaching and learning, studying and reflecting, in self-created ignorance of the world of politics, economics, commerce, and practical activity. There are no longer, if there ever were, any ivory towers, and those who seek such lofty retreats are being fundamentally irresponsible. For, whereas in the past, the issues of the day might have been issues simply for particular people in particular times and particular places, those issues that are distinctively contemporary have strikingly wider application. Many contemporary dilemmas are in a straightforward physical sense inescapable. Partly this stems from technological developments which are themselves a function of education and which have made apparently local concerns into global concerns.

No doubt the most pressing of contemporary issues is that of war, particularly nuclear war, with the question of nuclear proliferation a dominating consideration. Coming to terms with this problem is essentially a matter of global concern, for there are no refuges available from which it is possible to ignore the threat to continued life on the planet that is involved. But global threats of this nature are not confined to the contingency of war. Chemicals and pesticides manufactured in the developed world are exported to the Third World and return in contaminated products for the consumption of their originators. Modern technology, in other words, has shrunk the world to a size in which the concern of one is the concern of all.

Education, particularly in science and technology, that is blind to these issues and ignores the threat to continued existence on the planet that is involved, has an ostrich-like quality. Though it is possible for schools and educators to ignore these contemporary issues, doing so detracts from the nature of their occupation. Where educators have ignored such issues, their action has been based on a historical separating out over the course of the present century of factual questions from questions of value. This has partly been a product of the influence of logical positivism and the empiricist epistemology this involves, and partly a result of the gains made in sciences such as sociology and psychology by adopting quantitative and experimental methods—the triumph of the value-free ideal. And yet, paradoxically, it was scientists engaged in sciences with the minimum of social or ethical content, such as nuclear physics and quantum mechanics, who were first obliged to take account of the political and social implications of their factual discoveries when, in an unsuccessful attempt to prevent the exploding of the first atomic bomb, they quit the seclusion of their laboratories. It must be the case that education, no less than academic research, is worse for ignoring the moral dimensions of scientific advance and discovery.

There are other contemporary issues, though, that it is not merely undesirable but even impossible for the educator to ignore, since they are so much a part of the fabric of life that the school itself must adopt a position and a policy whether it wishes to do so or not. These are issues such as racism, sexism, separatism and secession, and personal and family relationships. Each of these issues, which are essentially moral issues, though with political and legal dimensions, requires resolution on an individual basis in terms of values and attitudes. And whatever theoretical position the individual embraces has its practical expression in behaviour. In particular, teachers' values and attitudes will be reflected in approaches and strategies within the classroom, while the attitudes and values of the wider society will be reflected in the structure of schooling and in practical arrangements which have a bearing on these fundamental issues.

It is easy to see this in the case of the first two issues identified. Schools with racial distinctions that are enforced by law belong to societies that are themselves structured on racial lines. But schools that are *de facto* divided on racial lines reflect a more subtle form of apartheid not confined to deliberately or overtly racist countries. The introduction of busing, particularly in the United States, can be seen as an attempt to counter this drift to a subtly racist form of educational organisation, though an attempt that cannot simply be considered on its merits from this point of view alone, since there are factors like parental choice and practical effects on the students concerned which need to be taken into account as well. Nevertheless, at the broadest level of the constitution and composition of schools, the issue of racism is not one that can be ignored by the educational system. Still less can it be ignored by the individual teacher for whom the need to adopt approaches within the classroom that convey equality of respect toward members of different racial groups is pressing. This requirement applies even where classes do not contain members of all racial groups, for discussion of literary, historical, or geographical topics provides involuntary and not always anticipated opportunities for the projection of either racist or nonracist attitudes.

The issue of racism intrudes into education in other ways, too. Debates about racial intelligence are naturally pertinent, and conclusions reached on this issue tend to be reflected in attitudes to reverse discrimination in selection procedures, particularly for higher education or professional training. The fact of differential racial performance on tests that are used for this purpose is in general conceded, with disagreement turning on the causal explanation.

Explanation in terms of genetic endowment is seen as racist in itself and as failing to justify policies of reverse discrimination. On the other hand, explanation in terms of social and environmental factors is viewed as being free of racist overtones and as distributing the blame for differential performance between the racial groups concerned, usually through explanations in terms of exploitation and socially produced economic and cultural deprivation. Since this appears to make differences artificial, it furnishes an *a priori* justification for allowing more generous terms for entry into higher education and the professions. In fact, of course, the type of causal factors involved is only important if some causes are more susceptible of alteration by human intervention than others. And where an individual is concerned, discriminatory assistance is likely to be offered only when the network of causation has already made that individual what he or she is and will, for better or worse, continue to be. Reverse discrimination, then, is vitiated by the fact that it is first, policy based on racial generalisations and second, an attempt to effect changes at too late a stage for individual members of racial groups to be usefully affected. Nevertheless, to secure adequate representation of members of different races in prestigious occupations, it may be necessary to proceed with some limited form of affirmative action despite its recognised inadequacies. And it is certainly the case that these are matters on which any educational institution is bound in practice to determine a policy and carry it through. Educational policies and race are inextricably interconnected.

In the same way, the issue of what has come to be termed *sexism* impinges on both classroom behaviour and educational organisation. In the classroom, first of all, sexual stereotyping may be imposed by the teacher's expectations and by the use of textbooks which thoughtlessly reinforce outdated expectations of male and female behaviour and occupations. This may include, for example, addressing significantly different types of questions to boys and girls or distributing leadership roles disproportionately to boys. Teachers who believe they do not have any particular attitude toward one sex rather than the other may find on objectively evaluating their procedures that they have, after all, taken up in practice conventional and traditional attitudes.

But organisational questions are also involved in this issue, with factual investigation of the consequences for both sexes of segregated or mixed schooling being ultimately the only thing that can determine which of these forms of organisation is best able to make a contribution to education that is in the best interests of both sexes.

Racism and sexism, then, are issues that inevitably intrude into the classroom and are also involved in the structure and shape of the educational system. Teachers and administrators are bound to take account of them. There are some issues, however, which do, in fact, intrude into many classrooms although they are not directly part and parcel of the process of education. Three in particular may be mentioned here.

Many school students become involved in political activities such as marches and demonstrations, which raise in an acute form questions of the limits of political action, the use of violence to achieve political ends, law and authority, and the role of the police. In practice, it is difficult for teachers to stand aside from these issues or to avoid taking up a particular stance in relation to issues which closely concern their students, perhaps even dominating their extracurricular lives. But opinion will be divided on what the teacher's role in these matters should be. Clearly some teachers who share the political outlook of their students will approve their activities and lend them tacit or open support. Others will see respect for authority and for conventional political tactics as something that teachers should aim to inculcate in their own students, and they will see the school situation as an opportunity to influence students in this direction. In either case, therefore, it is easy to see now what is strictly extracurricular may become inextricably involved in the school situation.

Certain other more localised political issues of our time may impinge on the classroom in a similar way to this, but with perhaps stronger and more direct consequences. These are particularly issues concerned with separatism and secession. Of these, particularly for students in the United Kingdom, the Northern Ireland situation is one of the most tragic and dominating examples, but separatist movements in other European countries, in Canada, and in many other parts of the world provide parallel examples. In all these cases, schools play a central part, not merely because children become enmeshed in the political activities of their parents and teachers—sometimes even as unwilling spectators of some of the gory internecine strife of their elders as the school itself becomes briefly a setting for murder, protest, or violent repression—but because national or ethnic identities and culture may provide an alternative content for education. Hence in particular, demands for teaching to take place in the language of the threatened culture generate important curriculum decisions, affecting, for example, the literature to be studied and history to be taught—decisions which go beyond a mere change of language. If religion, too, is involved, then the question may become one of alternative schools as well as an alternative culture, thus generating a further, yet more intractable, set of problems.

Finally, there is a range of issues of a more domestic nature, which for this reason must closely affect the lives of children and adolescents in school, and which, if ignored, may severely diminish the school's effectiveness. These are issues connected with the family, marriage, separation, and divorce—those personal and sexual relationships that form the stuff and fabric of existence for people in their domestic setting. In some schools, a majority of children will belong to one-parent families, and yet assumptions and attitudes of teachers and of the school as an organisation may be based on the traditional assumption of the two-parent family and conventional parental roles. Teachers will inevitably bring their own attitudes to bear on the problems that may be encountered by their students, and, as the teacher's pastoral role enlarges, the effects of this on more academic areas of education will become more significant.

So far, then, a range of issues that strikingly affect present times and present lives has been described. They are important problems, preeminently ethical, though with important social, political, and legal dimensions. They are not, of course, the only problems for contemporary society, and neither are they uniformly as difficult of solution. But it is useful to identify at least some of these problems and to consider them in relation to the enterprise of education. Initial identification of the problems shows them to have surprisingly direct connections with schools and with the task and role of the teacher. It remains to consider, then, to what extent this recognition involves acceptance of the political nature of education.

First, however, one further contemporary issue must be mentioned, since it is the one that has dominated most educational discussion and research in many Western countries and some Eastern European ones in recent years. This is the issue of social class. The goal of eliminating the class basis of society through reorganisation of the education system has consistently been presented in terms of increasing equality and equality of opportunity. Only recently has it been appreciated to what extent equality of opportunity is, in fact, incompatible with actual equality, and it is this goal that has begun to displace the more meritocratic conception of equalising opportunity.

The example deserves mentioning here, though, because it effectively illustrates the fact that certain problems and issues can only find resolution within education at the level of restructuring of the educational system itself. Others, by contrast, may effectively be treated by individual teachers at the classroom level, or at least within schools as units. The rooting out of social class distinctions, though, has throughout the present century commended itself in terms of a reconstituted educational system. At first, this was seen to mean open procedures of selection for differentiated education. More recently, this has been superseded by the advocacy of the elimination of selection and a common education.

This particular issue is marked out from the others that have so far been mentioned by the fact that it is distinctively political in a more partisan sense than any of the others. Sympathy or antipathy to social class distinctions is seen as an ideological stance indicating political allegiance on a right-left spectrum, and hence a matter of internal party politics. The other issues mentioned, though they may feature in one way or another in the programmes of political parties, have a universal aspect that suggests that they are problems for everyone and that their solution is itself a matter of searching for answers which can commend themselves to everybody. Party politics is too narrow a platform on which to resolve the issues of the age of technology, dominated as it is by political extremism and a general and pervading Machiavellianism in regard to morality. This is not to deny that political parties may set out for voters their preferred solutions and strategies; it is simply to acknowledge that in the face of threats to humanity as a whole, there is a sense in which the solutions advanced by particular political parties, whatever their aspirations, can only become operative by securing general and widespread agreement.

The issue of social class, then, is a narrower problem than the ones that have so far been identified. As far as these other, wider issues are concerned, the crucial question is whether there is any hope of solutions being arrived at through the medium of an education committed to common human values and universal human aspirations. But before the question of values can be considered, it must be asked whether it is possible to identify any common human aspirations. An immediate response to this question is generated by the observation that the first group of issues that were described here raise in a potent form the question of human survival, and it would be difficult to deny that the aspiration to survive is something that should have the potential of securing the widest possible human agreement. The second range of issues—those involved in questions of race and sex—again involve very widespread human aspirations, since they relate to the notions of human dignity and equality of respect that have been embodied in the universal declarations of rights to which most civilised nations are signatories. In itself this may mean little, for the gap between prevailing practice and official policy may provide room for a considerable wedge of cynicism to insert itself. Nevertheless, if it is aspirations that are in question, the willingness of nations to attempt to express these in a formal and agreed way provides at least a worthwhile starting point. And in the special case of education, it happens that there is a general agreement that it is idealism rather than cynicism that should carry the day, since these declarations actually include, in self-referential style, expressions of intent that the aspirations and agreements themselves should be communicated to students through the educational system.

The more controversial issues involved in the assertion of cultural identity and modes of political action are admittedly more capable of splitting person from person, teacher from teacher, student from student. Nevertheless, it might at least be agreed that their resolution is a common task, and the way in which revolutionary movements themselves have become increasingly international, their tendency to take up each other's local conflicts and supply aid, succour, and training to each other's members, suggests that the solution to these problems, too, must be sought on a scale that transcends the purely local and parochial.

Let it be admitted, then, that there are common human aspirations that are relevant to the issues which have been discussed here. The question remains as to whether solutions are to be found through the application of common human values—values which it can be the business of schools and educators to transmit and propagate. This is a wider question than any that have been raised so far. But it suggests, at least, that matters which initially seemed to be political may, in the end, be ethical—not partisan but universal. It is a question, however, that it may be possible to answer in a positive rather than a negative fashion. For a liberal and humanistic concept of education is itself a concept of education within which certain values are implicit. And if further investigation of these values shows them to be essentially universal in application, this at the same time establishes their relevance to the solution of the moral and practical dilemmas that have been considered here.

The nature of these values has already revealed itself to some extent in the course of the discussion. They include, of course, values of individual dignity—respect for a person as a person, the Kantian awareness of the need to treat all representatives of humanity as ends in themselves and not as exploitable objects. They include, too, the values of toleration, impartiality, and freedom of enquiry—all these at least partly justified by their effectiveness in producing solutions to practical problems through the medium of investigation, argument, and the unfettered use of reason.

But no values can be preserved without the preservation of humanity itself. Hence the value that is of greatest relevance in the face of contemporary issues and dilemmas is one that might be called in a much wider sense than this term in usually used, the value of paternalism. By this is meant the protective and caring impulse directed at securing the interest and the life itself of the present younger generation and of unborn future generations. Many of today's dominating issues are, in a sense never previously known, issues of survival. The ethical stance of caring and acting for survival is thus a value that could and should commend itself widely enough to provide a political direction for education which is truly, and in the widest possible sense, humanistic.

Finally, it must be asked whether education which is sensitive to these issues, which is politically future-oriented rather than past-ossified, generates the problems of teacher bias or neutrality that arise in the case of value education which is more particular and partisan. The answer to this question is that commitment to moral values that have the kind of breadth of appeal that has been suggested here is not bias in any derogatory sense. The lack of commitment to these values which is indicated by the concept of neutrality is, on the other hand, fundamentally objectionable. It is objectionable in the sense that contemporary problems demand a solution, and solutions are only to be found through commitment to the kind of ideals that a humanistic conception of education involves. Hence education and the contemporary issues that confront us are, for better or worse, inextricably interwoven. Hope lies in the fact that a solution may be pursued through morally aware educational processes. Only in this way can education become politically and socially relevant, without being used in a politically manipulative and instrumentalist way.

Notes

1. D. Hargreaves, *The Challenge for the Comprehensive School* (London: Routledge & Kegan Paul, 1982), p. 189.
2. Ibid., p. 184.
3. Ibid., p. 185.
4. Ibid., p. 226.
5. T. Pateman, *Language, Truth and Politics* (Lewes; E. Sussex: Jean Stroud, 1980), p. 170.
6. G. Partington, "Race Riots in England," *Quadrant* 25 (December 1981): 50; reprinted, *Bulletin* (London: National Council for Educational Standards, 1982).

8
Ethical Aspects of the Development of the Analytic Tradition

In these two essays I want to examine two aspects of the development of the analytic movement, in each case relating a particular epistemological stance to a particular ethical position. The two philosophers whose work I will take as examples of this kind of connection between epistemological and ethical views are G. E. Moore and A. J. Ayer, each of whom was influential in contributing a different strand to the development of the analytic movement in British philosophy.

G. E. Moore

EPISTEMOLOGY, ETHICS, AND COMMON SENSE

Moore set a particular pattern of analysis in epistemology that was later followed and developed by Austin and others, and employed as a method of argument appeal to the everyday uses of language. Moore himself might not have wished to be associated with the view that the analysis of ordinary language and study of its uses could evaporate philosophical problems, for undoubtedly he continued to see philosophical problems as problems to the end of his life. Also, he firmly denied that he was concerned with merely verbal, as opposed to conceptual, questions. Nevertheless, he attempted to find solutions in what he called common sense. And since ordinary language reflects commonsense assumptions, it is not surprising that it is the ordinary language strand in analytic philosophy to which his views seem to lead. As far as ethics is concerned, Moore's starting point was the examination of ethical language, so that it is arguable that it was his approach to ethics that set the pattern for what he went on to say about broader problems of knowledge rather than the other way about.

The basic position underlying both Moore's ethical and his epistemological ideas were two distinctions to which I shall return later. These two distinctions were between knowing and being able to prove, on the one hand, and between understanding and being able to give an analysis, on the other. These distinctions meant that a simple assertion of intuitive knowledge of the good was as justified for Moore in the area of ethics as were the simple epistemological claims of his "Defence of Common Sense."[1] But whereas in the case of the analysis of statements about material objects, Moore felt that he was never able satisfactorily to explain what he called relation R, the relation between sense-data and objects, or to render a wholly satisfactory analysis of a judgment of perception, in the case of the good, he found the problem of analysis satisfactorily solved by saying that the notion of the good did in fact represent the final stage of analysis and could not be subjected to any further breakdown or explanation. And just as he favoured an act-object analysis of perception, with the immediate "consciousness of blue" playing a crucial role, so in ethics he favoured an analysis in which the good provided the *object* of the *act* of intuition. If Moore could have convinced himself that the "consciousness of blue" provided a terminus to discussion equivalent to the intuitive recognition of good, then the debt that his epistemological views owed to his ethical views would have been even clearer.

Before looking in more detail at Moore's position, it would be useful to place his views in their historical context. It is a commmonplace that, before this century, moral philosophy was invariably conceived as a guide to moral conduct, and that it consisted of attempts to answer such questions as, what ought we to do? or, what is the good life? This view is borne out by consideration of the moral philosophy of Plato and Aristotle, by consideration of the ethical aspects of the Judaeo-Christian tradition, and even, with some qualification, of the in other respects revolutionary ideas of Kant. Moore's *Principia Ethica*, published in 1903, heralded a complete change of emphasis. From this point on, and until very recently, the task for moral philosophy was seen by philosophers within the analytic tradition as being to expose the essential meaning of moral words, to determine or categorise the nature of moral judgements. This applied both to the intuitionist/objectivist position of G. E. Moore and to the attitudinal accounts of ethics that followed from applying the basic principles of logical positivism to ethics and moral language.

Within the analytic tradition, there are accounts that accept the basic subject-predicate form in which many moral judgements are couched as nonmisleading, and that define moral characteristics in terms of other characteristics, either empirical or nonempirical. Following Moore's usage, the first can be described as naturalistic analyses and include such influential theories as utilitarianism, and the second can be called nonnaturalistic analyses. Nonnaturalists, however, become indistinguishable in their basic position from intuitionists (such as Prichard, Ross, and Ewing), the difference being simply that the latter tend to emphasise moral judgements of the form "one ought to do x" rather than following the form "x is good," which is favoured by nonnaturalists, a term that includes Moore himself. This means that while intuitionists ground ethics on the sense of moral obligation, nonnaturalists ground it on recognition of an objective moral quality, such as the "good." The common feature of such views, whether intuitionist or nonnaturalist, is that they make moral judgements ultimate and self-supporting. No further court of appeal is allowed beyond the immediate recognition that a particular state of affairs or general situation is good or bad, or a particular type of action right or wrong. Although this view offers security to those able to accept it, by its very nature it offers no external support for those inclined to doubt it.

In what follows, I should like to discuss this direction for ethics as set by Moore and then, in the second half of this chapter, contrast it with those theories within the analytic tradition that did not assume that the analysis of moral judgements was to be based on acceptance of the subject-predicate form in which many moral judgements are cast. Principally, the challenge to this acceptance came from the emotive and expressionist theories of ethics, one influential ground for which was logical positivism, that are characterised by an emphasis on the essentially prescriptive rather than descriptive function of moral discourse.

But before considering the details of Moore's ethical position, something must be said about his general philosophical stance, and, in particular, about what it was that Moore, at the time of writing *Principia Ethica* was reacting *against*. Both G. E. Moore and Bertrand Russell, together at Cambridge at the turn of the century, were concerned to reverse the effects of the prevailing philosophical climate by countering the metaphysical preoccupations of the nineteenth century. In this way, they anticipated positivism by reactivating the empiricist tradition in British philosophy but adding to it the element of analysis. The prevailing concern of the young Moore and Russell in the opening years of the century was to introduce science, precision, and light where metaphysics had, in their opinion, produced darkness, confusion, and the denial of the validity of sense-experience and common sense. In his intellectual autobiography, Russell wrote of himself and Moore: "He [G. E. Moore] took the lead in rebellion, and I followed, with a sense of emancipation. Bradley argued that everything common sense believes in is mere appearance; we reverted to the opposite extreme, and thought that *everything* is real that common sense, uninfluenced by philosophy or theology, supposes real. . . . The world which had been thin and logical, suddenly became rich and varied and solid."[2]

Neither Russell nor Moore were able to maintain this simple position for very long, but it remained Moore's objective to defend the beliefs of common sense whatever the philosophical difficulties. As far as the reception and effects of Moore's ethical views were concerned, however, he was not in fact seen by his contemporaries as championing the moral point of view of the ordinary person. Instead, his views were taken up with quite remarkable enthusiasm by people whose own approach to morality was very different from prevailing views. These included literary figures such as Virginia Woolf, Leonard Woolf, and Rupert Brooke, as well as the economist, John Maynard Keynes.

On Moore's chapter "The Ideal" in *Principia Ethica*, Keynes wrote: "I know no equal to it in literature since Plato because it is quite free from fancy. It conveys the beauty of the literalness of Moore's mind, the pure and passionate intensity of his vision, unfanciful and undressed up."[3]

And Lytton Strachey wrote to Moore in what can only be considered extravagant terms:

> I think your book has not only wrecked and shattered all writers on Ethics from Aristotle and Christ to Herbert Spencer and Mr. Bradley; it has not only laid the true foundations of Ethics, it has not only left all modern philosophy bafouée—these seem to me small achievements compared to the establishment of that Method which shines like a sword between the lines. It is the scientific method deliberately applied, for the first time to Reasoning. . . . I date from October 1903 the beginning of the Age of Reason.[4]

Exaggerated or not, it is the "scientific method applied to reasoning" that I wish to examine here, comparing its results in Moore's epistemology with its results in his ethical theory.

MOORE'S METHOD

Moore's characteristic method in tackling all types of philosophical problems was to take one or two statements that seemed to be implied by the philosophical positions involved, and then to show that these statements conflict with certain commonsense premises. His characteristic assumption is that if you can't *prove* your premise, it doesn't mean you don't *know* it. Also, that there are many propositions of which we know the meaning in the sense of *understanding* them, but that we do not know in the sense of being able to give an *analysis* of them. That is, Moore draws two distinctions: (1) between "knowing" and "being able to prove"; and (2) between "understanding" and "being able to give an analysis."

Applying these distinctions to philosophical problems, Moore would hold that one may know that a certain material object exists without being able to prove that it does, and may understand what it means to say that it does, without being able to give an analysis of it. In ethics, one may know that for example, human love is good without being able to prove that it is, and one may understand what this means without being able to give an analysis of it.

Moore thinks that if a philosopher thinks he can prove that something we know (e.g., that material objects exist) is not so, he must be wrong; and secondly, that if any philosopher offers an analysis of such a statement that would entail that any statement we know to be true is false, then it is his analysis that must be at fault, not our knowledge or our understanding.

"A Defence of Common Sense" provides a good example of this method applied to nonethical problems. Moore begins his essay with an outline of the commonsense views he wishes to defend. They are, first, his own beliefs about his body, its continous spatial existence on the earth since his birth, his knowledge of the existence of other bodies, his perception of objects and of facts about objects, and secondly, the belief that knowledge of these things as applied to themselves is common to at least very many other human beings; that is, that many other human beings believe about themselves what he believes about himself. Moore insists that these types of propositions can be known to be true. Whereas idealists or metaphysicians argue that they cannot be true because the assumption that they are true leads to incompatible conclusions, Moore insists that while these propositions could not be true if they *did* entail incompatible conclusions, since they *are* true, they cannot lead to incompatible conclusions. Any argument that suggests that they do, then, must be more doubtful than the limpid certainty with which common sense is able to assert them. The same point is made even more emphatically in Moore's "Proof of an External World"—a lecture in which Moore is said to have shocked some of his audience by holding up two hands as proof that there are (at least two) physical objects.

But in "A Defence of Commonsense," he goes on to raise the different question of the analysis of propositions about material things. And at this point, he introduces a very non-commonsense theory of representative perception, according to which we do not directly perceive material objects but instead a related sense-datum. A *sense-datum* is explained as something we are inclined to identify with a part of the surface of the object, but on reflection realise it cannot be this, since if the sense-datum were actually a part of the object, we would have to accept the fact that the same part would appear differently to different people, and to the same person under varying conditions. Also, Moore thought cases of illusion, such as seeing double, make it necessary to conclude that sense-data cannot be identical with the object or part of the object.

The relation, though, that must exist between the object and the sense-datum is difficult to explain. The view that it is an ultimate and unanalysable relation is open to the objection that we cannot possibly *know* that one thing stands in this relation to the sense-datum in question, and also that we could not know anything about such a thing even if we knew it to exist.

Moore's conclusion, then, is that the proposition that there are material things is true, but has not yet been satisfactorily analysed. The view of those philosophers he is concerned to refute, on the other hand, is that they have, by their analysis of the proposition, shown either that it is false or that it is unknowable.

As far as these philosophers are concerned, of course, whether Moore has successfully refuted them or not depends on the correctness of his interpretation of their view. Moore treats "There are no material objects" as an empirical assertion, arguing that it cannot be a logically necessary proposition since its denial is not self-contradictory. Moore did not feel it could be taken, either, as merely a linguistic recommendation. On the other hand, it is difficult to take it as an empirical observation if *empirical* is taken to mean "verifiable by sense-experience," since it is essentially the denial that sense-experience can verify. The philosopher who denies the existence of chairs is not seeking more reliable guidance as to where he can sit down, although Moore sometimes gave the impression that he believed this was the case.

The technique of analysis employed in the case of perception, which involves quitting the argument at an ultimate and unanalysable relation, closely resembles the method that Moore employed, with considerably more success, in ethics.

Where perception was concerned, Moore had argued that the mistake of idealism lay in equating blue, or yellow, with the *sensation* of blue or yellow, or with consciousness of blue or yellow. In "The Refutation of Idealism," he argued that it was necessary to distinguish the *act* of sensing from its object.[5] His argument was simply that the same act, consciousness (colour awareness), is involved in recognising different objects—blue, yellow, and so on. So, since there is something that varies and something that stays the same in these different perceptions, he insisted that perception involves two things, both act and object. Having a sensation of blue is being aware of something blue.

In ethics, it is no mere coincidence that Moore compares the intuition of good to the perception of yellow, and uses this as a justification for his own form of ethical objectivism. Just as he will not allow perception to be reduced by idealists to sensations alone, so he denies any ethical analysis that reduces ethical awareness to feeling alone. Ethical intuition must have a real object just as much as sense-perception.[6]

For Moore, *good* is the ultimate ethical term, with *right* and *ought* dependent on it. Moore's explanation of *good* depends on distinguishing first of all between complex and simple properties. Both *yellow* and *good* are examples of simple properties, neither of them being capable of further analysis or breaking down into constituent elements. Simple properties are then divided by Moore into *natural* properties which can be perceived directly by the senses or by introspection, for example, yellow, sweet; and *nonnatural* properties, which are like yellow in being simple and indefinable, but are not perceived by the senses. The sole example of this is *good*.[7]

A natural quality, then, is one that is either perceived by the senses (like yellow) or by introspection (like pleasantness). The faculty by which we are supposed to be aware of nonnatural properties is one of nonsensuous intuition. If anyone claims to have knowledge through this medium, they can hardly be refuted. It cannot be *proved* that people do not have faculties that are undetectable to perceive properties that are unobservable, if they claim that they do. But the usual dilemma of any form of intuitionism will arise when many people claiming this faculty report conflicting results of their intuitings.

One might say that good is so different in kind from other qualities as to make it unreasonable to call it a quality at all. And, in fact, it adds nothing to the description of a thing to say that it is good; neither do objects differ from each other solely in the fact that one is good and another bad. "Good" is evidently the verdict passed on the complete object, not a further property of it.[8]

Moore's theory about the nature of good raises, then, a number of problems. It was, however, this theory that provided the basis of the ethical argument for which he is best known—the argument concerning the Naturalistic Fallacy.[9]

THE NATURALISTIC FALLACY

By *naturalism*, Moore meant the identification of a moral term like *good* with some natural property. A naturalistic property was a characteristic the presence of which could be ascertained empirically either by observation or by introspection. For example:

good = more evolved; good = pleasant; good = commanded by those in authority

This kind of identification was what Moore termed the naturalistic fallacy. His argument may be summarized as follows:

Someone offers a definition or analysis of good:
Good = D (def.)
Then to ask: "Is D good?" is to ask a significant question.

This cannot, therefore, be equivalent to "Is D D?"

For example, "Is what represents a later stage of evolution good?" is not equivalent to the tautologous "Is what represents a later stage of evolution representative of a later stage of evolution?" Frankena, indeed, has argued that the Naturalistic Fallacy is really a subspecies of the definist fallacy, which consists simply of confusing or identifying two different properties.[10] But defining and analysing are not necessarily the same thing, and Moore would certainly have distinguished them. *Defining* sounds a purely verbal operation, something to be carried out with the help of a dictionary, and Moore was clear that his conception of analysis was *not* purely verbal. Whether *defining* or *analysing* is the term used, Moore claimed that the subject was a concept and not a verbal expression. In fact he offered three conditions for "giving an analysis" of a concept. These were:

1. that both analysandum and analysans must be concepts—the *same* one, if the analysis is correct,
2. that two different *expressions* must be used, and
3. the analysans must *explicitly mention* concepts not mentioned in the analysandum.

"A brother is a male sibling" meets these requirements, and the proposition can be translated into other languages without confusion, thus showing that it is concepts rather than verbal expressions that are involved.[11]

On this account, the *possibility* of analysing *good* would remain open, if it were not for Moore's other arguments about the simplicity of the notion. It may be, though, that in the Naturalistic Fallacy argument, Moore is simply pointing to the error of identifying the ethical with the nonethical, in which case he is not indicating a *logical* fallacy at all. Frankena suggests that in order to know any kind of mistake is involved in definitions of *good* or other moral terms you need to know beforehand that these qualities *are* nonnatural and indefinable. Only then can you accuse the would-be definer of a mistake in terms of Moore's argument. So Moore's position really amounts to the familiar intuitionist claim that there are moral properties. And failing to recognise moral properties is not committing a *fallacy* but is, in fact, a kind of moral blindness if there *are* such things as moral properties. On the other hand, of course, if there are no such things as moral properties, then thinking you can detect them is to be the victim of moral hallucination.

As in the case of arguments about the existence of material objects and the problem of perception, it is necessary to see Moore here as attempting to defend the commonsense view of the situation against philosophical sophistication. A realist defence of material objects corresponds to an intuitionist claim of the real existence of moral properties. But where it is clear that in the case of the epistemological issue no real disagreement exists about appropriate human responses to what might be called the "facts" of the case—there is general agreement, for example, about approaching hard objects with caution rather than attempting to propel one's body through them—there *is* genuine disagreement about the appropriate responses to facts of ethical significance.

So while phenomenalists, causal theorists, and realists can continue to dispute the *analysis* of statements about material objects while behaving in the same way toward them, there is a sense in which the intuitionist position put forward by Moore denies differences of opinion that do actually exist. This is, of course, a general point about any kind of intuitionist position, not just Moore's, and it is worth noticing that intuitionists differ in what it is they apply their intuition to. Moore applied it to states of affairs and it is these to which the term *good* can most naturally be applied. This explains why Moore is sometimes classed as an Ideal Utilitarian. As opposed to claiming that we should follow any *principles* of action, he argued that we should consider the possible consequences of our actions—something that must inevitably leave room for doubt—and choose to bring about the one that contains the maximum of good.[12] Other intuitionists have held that certain classes of actions or moral principles such as promise keeping or truth telling are what we recognise as right or morally obligatory without further argument or calculation. And still others have seemed to suggest that we can see what is our duty on particular occasions in particular situations.

In general, these claims, while seeming to confer high status on ethical considerations, in fact remove the possibility of serious and rational ethical debate. In commenting on Moore's announced concern for "the fundamental principles of ethical reasoning," Geoffrey Warnock writes: "It is curious that his conclusion is really that there are no such principles. For on questions about goodness he has no place for reasoning at all, while on questions of what is right there is purely causal or inductive enquiry into the consequences of action, of a kind that we might engage in without any moral interest whatever."[13]

The fact that people do disagree on moral issues is not the only objection to the intuitionist position, although it is probably the most important. It is also the case that those forms of intuitionism that attempt to recognise principles must also come to terms with the fact that in some situations, different moral principles will be in conflict with each other. It is not invariably possible, for instance, to be both kind and truthful, to save lives and keep promises, or even to prevent suffering and not to kill. So for some intuitionists, it becomes important to devise a hierarchy of principles, or to turn to the claim that moral duties are obvious in individual situations—a very counterintuitive claim outside closed circles of like-minded friends or colleagues.

These points do not apply, though, to Moore's form of intuitionism, which was characterised by its rejection of rigid principles and, indeed, for this very reason had the appeal it did to literary figures (for example, the members of the Bloomsbury group mentioned earlier) who rejected the rigid conventions of their time. Moore himself was far from drawing these unconventional conclusions, but the aspect of *Principia Ethica* which impressed at least some of Moore's nonphilosophical contemporaries was not his theory about the good or his exposure of the Naturalistic Fallacy, but the chapter which he called "The Ideal."[14]

In this he explicitly asserted his view that the question "What ought we to do?" is an empirical question since it is a matter of what (causally) produces good things. Moore goes on to draw the conclusion that since this can only be a matter of probability, it is better to aim at goods affecting oneself and close friends rather than attempting extended benevolence, because one is more likely to be certainly effective in a narrower sphere. For the same reason, he claimed that it is better to aim at immediate rather than more distant satisfactions. His answer to the question, "What is good in itself?" was: "Certain states of consciousness which may be roughly described as the pleasures of human intercourse and the enjoyment of beautiful objects." In other words, personal affection and aesthetic appreciation. This is a material and emotional ideal. It is not a spiritual ideal, and it is also interesting that it leaves out intellectual objectives or ideals such as knowledge and truth that might have been expected of a philosopher of Moore's type.

Moore's type, then, and Moore's style was that of a philosopher concerned with questions of analysis. In ethics, his deviation in the direction of saying what kind of things he saw as having intrinsic value—intrinsic goodness—may be seen as, although influential, in some ways inconsistent with the extreme austerity of his position. This position, in both epistemology and ethics, consisted in holding out high hopes for analysis, but in the end failing to deliver anything that could stand up to challenge. Moore always distinguished questions like "Are there material objects?" from the epistemological question "Can anyone know that there are material objects?" and in the end he was obliged to counter the extreme scepticism that resulted from his failure to produce satisfactory analyses in response to the second kind of question with assertions of certainty about the answer to the first. In both ethics and epistemology, this required the importation of some special kind of faculty or awareness that could be seen as resistant to philosophical argument. In epistemology, common sense was summoned to fulfil this requirement; in ethics, it was nonsensuous intuition. Subsequent philosophers in the analytic tradition cut adrift from these moorings and started out on more uncharted seas. Their direction had, though, to a considerable extent been set by Moore and by the analytic technique he initiated.

A. J. Ayer

In *Language, Truth and Logic*, Ayer wrote: "We shall set ourselves to show that in so far as statements of value are significant, they are ordinary 'scientific' statements; and that in so far as they are not scientific, they are not in the literal sense significant, but are simply expressions of emotion which can be neither true nor false."[15]

It is this theory that I shall be discussing here, at the same time relating it to the wider positivist position. First, though, it may be of some interest to mention the connection between Moore and Ayer. Ayer remains an admirer of Moore and acknowledges a debt to him. This debt seems least considerable in the area of ethics, and yet, according to Ayer's own account in his autobiography, it was Moore's ethical theories that formed the first point of contact between them. It was while he was still at school that Ayer read Clive Bell's book an art in which, in a chapter entitled "Art and Ethics," Bell wrote of Moore: "I have no mind by attempting to reproduce his dialectic to incur the merited ridicule of those familiar with *Principia Ethica* or to spoil the pleasure of those who will be wise enough to run out this very minute and order a masterpiece with which they happen to be unacquainted."[16]

Ayer records that he obeyed this instruction and became an equally ardent convert to Moore's ethical views, only coming to doubt whether "good" was an indefinable nonnatural quality during his undergraduate years at Oxford. But the ethical position that Ayer ultimately adopted was the emotive theory of ethics, which is so succinctly summed up in the opening quotation. This derives not from the influence of Moore, but from the positivism of the Vienna Circle, with which Ayer became acquainted in Vienna in 1932–33, and which provided the inspiration for *Language, Truth and Logic*. The Vienna Circle had formed around Moritz Schlick in the 1920s on, and included such figures as Waismann, Carnap, Neurath, Feigl, and Gödel. Wittgenstein was not actually a member but had some influence on the group (the *Tractatus* was published in 1921).

The group was science- and logic-oriented, and had as a primary goal the exclusion of metaphysics. This had obvious implications for ethics. Positivism limited meaningful statements to two categories: analytic statements that were true in virtue of the meaning of the terms involved (which is to say that if true, they were truistically true), and empirical statements, to the truth or falsity of which some sense-observation must be relevant. To some extent, this can be seen as a linguistic restatement of the essential position of empiricism as put forward in a much-quoted rhetorical passage in Hume: "If we take in our hand any volume; of divinity, or school metaphysics, for instance; let us ask, *Does it contain any abstract reasoning concerning quantity or number? No. Does it contain any experimental reasoning concerning matter of fact and existence?* No. Commit it then to the flames: for it can contain nothing but sophistry and illusion."[17]

Logical positivism provides a twentieth-century restatement of Hume's denunciation of attempts to stray beyond these boundaries. The claim that all knowledge other than that of logic is derived from experience is restated in the form of an assertion that all meaningful statements, other than those of logic and mathematics, are verifiable by reference to experience. It is sometimes said that this stems from Wittgenstein's remark in the *Tractatus* that "to understand a proposition means to know what is the case if it is true," although Wittgenstein himself is said to have denied that he intended to put forward a theory of meaning with this assertion.[18]

There are, of course, many general difficulties of verificationism, so much so that it has been called a "dead dogma." It has been pointed out that some concepts are not derived from experience, but are logically prior to experience. It has also been pointed out that verificationism is defective as a theory of meaning because meaning must be presupposed in applying the verifiability test. Again, there are problems about the status of the verification principle itself, which appears to be neither a tautology nor an empirical generalisation (though here there are possible answers such as that of Wittgenstein that philosophy is enlightening nonsense, or that of Schlick, that the verification principle is a truism). But most relevant here is the point that the exclusion of metaphysics seems only attainable by strategies that exclude other more useful categories of statement as well: those of science, for instance, because they make open-ended claims about the future, those of religion, and, most particularly, those of ethics.[19]

Ethical utterances have not, in general been held to be analytic— although Kant held that they were necessary and could be known *a priori*. The view that they are empirical is the naturalism that was dismissed by Moore as fallacious. And here it is interesting to note that Ayer used an argument to refute empirical or naturalistic interpretations of ethics that was in fact the inverted mirror image of Moore's argument against naturalism. Where Moore had argued that it is not a tautology to assert that any natural quality proposed as a definition of good is itself good, Ayer, in *Language, Truth and Logic* and again later in "The Analysis of Moral Judgements" employed the argument that it is not self-contradictory to deny any such equation.

This underlines an essential similarity of viewpoint between emotivism and intuitionism that it would be easy to overlook. For both converge in the view that where ultimate disagreement occurs on ethical matters, it is feeling rather than reason that must provide the final arbiter, though the feeling involved for the intuitionist is an intuitive recognition of some moral quality rather than subjective sentiment. No problem arises for either in conceding that there is much scope for factual argument and for causal and other forms of practical reasoning up to the point of an ultimate ethical judgement. And both concur in the view that at this point, reasoning gives out.

It is interesting to compare this with the situation in regard to an epistemological issue like perception. Whereas Moore attempted to remain firm at the level of insisting on the existence of material objects, though at the same time suggesting an analysis of the notion that ultimately led to phenomenalism, Ayer, in embracing the notion of sense-data (and, later, sense qualia) showed an apparent willingness to abandon a naive realist position. Nevertheless, in what he conceded and what he denied, his epistemological position was not nearly as far from that of Moore as might appear. In other words, just as in ethics, an intuitionist and an emotivist position are indistinguishable at the most fundamental level, so in epistemology the type of realism defended by Moore and the phenomenalism so frequently implied by Ayer have much in common. Ayer's phenomenalism is Moore's realism cut free from an essentially metaphysical faith in the real object. Ayer's emotivism is Moore's intuitionism cut free from the metaphysical assertion of the good. Without these two anchors, Moore offers nothing but subjective sensation or feeling, either in relation to material objects or in relation to ethical properties.

Inevitably, abandoning these anchors is a step in the direction of scepticism, for to be confined to one's feelings where standard epistemological issues are concerned is to risk being trapped in a solipsistic universe. This danger was only too familiar to the logical positivists who offered varying escape routes from it—a common structure to compensate for incommunicability of content, for instance, (Schlick) or intersubjectively verifiable "protocol statements" in the context of behaviourism or physicalism (Carnap), or simply coherence and acceptability to the scientists of our culture circle (Carnap again). Ayer's own philosophical contributions characteristically take the form of attempts to refute scepticism—about physical objects, about other minds, about causation. Indeed, it almost seems that it is only where the ethical consequences of his position were concerned that he was content to accept sceptical conclusions. A failure to refute scepticism in the epistemological case results in the kind of schizophrenia confessed to by Hume, in which the conclusions reached in the philosopher's study cannot withstand emergence into the world of light, life, and friendship. Ethical scepticism, though, has less overtly disturbing consequences.

However, just as Ayer has consistently denied that a phenomenalist theory of perception does necessarily involve scepticism about the material objects of common sense, so he has also strongly denied that the emotive analysis and subsequent more subtle attitudinal analyses of ethics involve moral scepticism or inertia. It is worth recording that as a private person, if not as a philosopher, Ayer has been associated with many movements for moral reform and has adopted a public stance on a variety of ethical issues. Nevertheless, the logical positivist position does involve a divorce between philosophy and this kind of moral stance.

Not only was this so, but Ayer's brief treatment of ethics in *Language, Truth and Logic* suggests that the loss of a rational ethics along with metaphysics and religion was not something he saw at that stage much reason to regret. Since ethical language was clearly *used*—it had a function—it could not be abandoned altogether as it was intended that metaphysics should be. Rejecting the notion that ethics could be reduced to any empirical concepts for much the same reason as Moore and rejecting, too, any absolutist interpretation of ethics, Ayer put the alternative view he favoured in these terms:

> We begin by admitting that the fundamental ethical concepts are unanalysable. . . . We say that the reason why they are unanalysable is that they are mere pseudo-concepts. The presence of an ethical symbol in a proposition adds nothing to its factual content. Thus if I say to someone "You acted wrongly in stealing that money" I am not stating anything more than if I had simply said "You stole that money." In adding that this action is wrong I am not making any further statement about it. I am simply evincing my moral disapproval of it.[20]

He goes on to say a little later: "In every case in which one would commonly be said to be making an ethical judgement, the function of the relevant ethical word is purely 'emotive.' It is used to express feeling about certain objects, but not to make any assertion about them." He adds: "It is worth mentioning that ethical terms do not serve only to express feeling. They are calculated also to arouse feeling and so to stimulate action."[21]

This analysis had been hinted at by earlier writers. Ogden and Richards had written in *The Meaning of Meaning* in 1923: "The peculiar ethical use of 'good' is, we suggest, a purely emotive use."[22] And they had contrasted the scientific use of language with the emotive use. C. D. Broad, in an article in the *Proceedings of the Aristotelian Society* for 1933–34 had suggested as an analysis of a statement about a self-sacrificing act being good: "That's an act of self-sacrifice. Hurrah!"[23]

The Swedish philosopher A. Hägerström had also independently advanced a noncognitivist view of ethics in "On the truth of moral propositions," which was published in 1911. There he wrote that "a proposition that a certain action represents a supreme value—cannot be said to be either true or false."[24] Again, the American philosopher C. L. Stevenson, who was also a leading exponent of the emotive theory, may have drawn his inspiration from other sources.[25]

Ayer, however, like Carnap, Schlick, and others, presented the theory as part of a deduction from the basic principles of logical positivism, and it is his critique of ethics in *Language, Truth and Logic* that constitutes the best-known brief exposition of emotivism.

In its original form, the theory was open to many objections, and, in particular, was felt to contradict the generally shared experience and convictions of people in regard to their interpersonal relationships. The theory was, for instance, apparently entirely particular. It demanded no continuity of moral conviction—the same person could condemn at three o'clock what he had praised at two o'clock. The theory did not imply any need for consistency of application either, so that the emotive analysis on its own supplied no reason why it should be thought odd for someone to maintain that an action was right for himself but wrong for Richard or Sarah, or wrong for himself but right for Peter, or indeed any other permutation. And thirdly, the theory did not seem to distinguish between individual moral judgements, such as "stealing this copy of *Principia Ethica* from this bookshop would be wrong" and "stealing is wrong," the same analysis apparently applying to either.

However, Ayer later came to the defence of his theory on several occasions, and the same basic position has been held and expanded by others. If we are to accept the strength of these theories in isolating the essential prescriptive elements of ethical language, it will be of interest to mention briefly some of the arguments later used by Ayer in support of the emotive analysis in "On the Analysis of Moral Judgements," since these avoid many of the difficulties of the original formulation.

Ayer begins by insisting that his early position was essentially correct in that ethical statements do not state facts in the way in which other empirical statements state facts. So, since this difference is undeniable, it is simply a matter of terminology whether they are to be accorded the status of facts demanded for them by objectivists.

For the unconvinced, Ayer suggests consideration of a case in which a murder has been committed. A recital of facts will include such details as when and where the killing took place; by what means; the identity of the murderer and of his victim. Conceivably, psychological and medical facts might be included in addition. But no account of the facts, however detailed, will include the information that the killing was right or wrong, morally justified or unjustified, since this type of statement functions as a *verdict on* the facts, and not as an addition to them.[26] What is more, two people may agree on all the facts and still disagree on the ethical judgement.

As for those who claim, like Moore, that moral judgements involve a reference to a different kind of fact—the presence or absence of nonempirical objective moral properties, Ayer argued that this type of theory, in making moral judgements descriptive, would defeat its own purpose by robbing the moral judgement of its more important aspect: the dynamic quality that entails that moral judgements do have implications for action. Ayer comments:

> A valuation is not a description of something very peculiar; it is not a description at all, ... Talking about values is not a matter of describing what may or may not be there, the problem being whether it really is there. There is no such problem. The moral problem is: What am I to do? What attitude am I to take? And moral judgements are directives in this sense.[27]

As a final argument, he urges that even if the objectivist could find objective values against which to check his own values, he would still be able to ask: But are these the real values or, in other words, are the things that I value really valuable?

This is not, Ayer urges, an argument that morals are unimportant, since this would itself be a moral position. Instead, it is an attempt to show what making a moral judgement essentially *is*, and is therefore *neutral* as regards any particular moral position. Ayer reiterates that saying that moral judgements are not statements of fact and cannot be true or false is not to say that nothing is good or bad, right or wrong. Again, this too would be a moral position—that of living without any policy. Neither is it to say that a thing is right if someone thinks it is, wrong if someone else thinks it is. The first "right," Ayer points out, is a reference to the speaker's own moral viewpoint. It may be that the notion expressed is, in fact, an attempt to formulate a principle of universal moral tolerance, but in this case, again, it would express a moral position. The theory itself remains, in spite of all these misinterpretations, neutral.

It is not, though, as completely particular and arbitrary as it seems. Ayer himself uses language that suggests an appeal to something wider and more general:

> An action or a situation is morally evaluated always as an action or a situation of a certain kind. What is approved or disapproved is something repeatable. In saying that Brutus or Raskolnikov acted rightly, I am giving myself and others leave to imitate them should similar circumstances arise. I show myself to be favourably disposed in either case towards actions of that type. Similarly, in saying that they acted wrongly, I express a resolution not to imitate them, and endeavour also to discourage others.[28]

The operative words and phrases here are the terms *imitate*; *repeatable*; *situations of a certain kind*; *actions of that type*; *similar circumstances*. Taken together, they imply a strong reference to the notion of pattern.

This notion of pattern is essentially a matter more commonly discussed in ethics as the universalisability of "ought." And although emphasis on this universal feature of ethical language is usually associated with opposition to, and refutation of, the emotive theory of ethics, the reference to a pattern of condemnation or approval implicit in remarks such as those of Ayer in "On the Analysis of Moral Judgements" essentially leads toward some such notion as this. It is, in any event, a logical, rather than ethical, notion of this type that is needed to complement the theory.

That emotivism can be modified and improved by developing the notion of universalisability is suggested by subsequent events. R. M. Hare advanced the theory known as prescriptivism that is built on recognising both the element of prescription that is already implicit within emotivism, and also the element of universality that it neglected. Hare's position is argued for on logical rather than moral grounds although it is sometimes confused with the moral position that everyone is entitled to equal consideration or with the moral rule: Do as you would be done by. It is a contemporary fallacy to suppose that there can be moral rules that apply only to oneself. Emotivism is an ethical theory that fits with such a quasi-existentialist position because it seems to imply that there can be duties that apply just to one person in one situation and have no wider application even in principle. Emotivism might seem then, to imply a certain kind of unique instance morality. However, Ayer himself was careful to read into the notion of an ethical attitude something of much wider application than this.

He was also careful to free himself of association with another fallacy—that of appearing to recommend universal moral toleration. For he recognised that in adopting any particular moral position, a person is necessarily implicitly condemning or at least dissociating himself from alternative and incompatible moral positions.

Indeed, few of the charges brought against the emotive theory of ethics can be maintained in the face of subtle adaptations of this kind, and some criticisms, like those just mentioned, are undoubtedly based on logical misconceptions. Nevertheless, there would be general agreement that the theory overemphasises the *function* of moral language and defines this function in a way that fails to distinguish it from such nonmoral techniques as propaganda and advertising. The function it emphasises is, in any case, not always present where ethical language is used, for there is a place for cool assessment of moral matters that the term *emotive* negates. It is usually pointed out, in any case, that attitudes, which is what are involved here, are very different from emotions, more substantial, secure, and lasting.

The strength of the theory, and an aspect that Hare took up and developed, was its recognition of the dynamism of moral terms, and yet even where this is concerned, it is not clear that ethical judgements invariably have dynamic force. For example, judgements that have no implications for present-day moral choices are made about historical or literary figures.

Finally, it is often suggested that the theory eliminates moral disagreement by turning ethical dispute into a matter of taste. This is a more serious charge and in "Man as a Subject for Science," Ayer shows himself disposed to a form of determinism that would, in effect, make ethical judgements a kind of aesthetic judgement.[29] This is a serious charge, for if morality is to be possible, humans must be recognised as agents, not merely the passive puppets of forces that shape and determine their responses to all situations. And yet, logical positivism was undoubtedly deterministic in its original and fundamental conception of reducing all sciences—which included, of course, the science of psychology—to one. But the position implied in Ayer's essay—that to try to draw a line between man and the rest of nature as a subject for science is to attempt the improbable if not the impossible—is open to one striking counterconsideration. This is that, improbable or not, man is at least unique in being able to raise and consider questions like these.

Whatever Ayer's ultimate conclusions on the wider issue of determinism—and elsewhere he offers a solution in terms of a contrast between causality and constraint[30]—there is no doubt that he has never seen either this or the ethical analysis he was prepared to adopt as a reason for opting out of the world of substantial ethical choice. In another essay on "Philosophy and Politics," he laments the failure of the analytic tradition to contribute to contemporary political debate in the way that alternative philosophies such as those of Sartre or Marx have done.[31] He writes with approval of Sartre's demand that philosophers should be committed (*engagés*) and its implication that philosophers should not only have views on political and social issues but that they should give their views a philosophical backing.

In these reflections, Ayer was anticipating the recent trend in ethics (particularly in America) away from questions of analysis to discussion of substantive ethical issues. In view of this, it is interesting that Ayer has shown increasing willingness to comment on public issues, writing, for example, in the London *Times* about the case of a doctor put on trial in the United Kingdom for bringing about the death of a very severely handicapped newborn baby by failing to intervene with medical techniques that could have saved its life. A willingness to offer a philosophical contribution to such a debate as well as to become, as Ayer did in 1982, the founding president of the Society for Applied Philosophy, is a long way from the dissociation between ethical theory and practice implied by the critique of ethics in *Language, Truth and Logic*.

The point is, essentially, as Hare and others have noticed, that even if ethical analysis were indisputably to show that moral judgements are a matter of competing volitions, volitions are themselves as legitimate an area for critical analysis and evaluations as anything else. The chief enemy of such a critical analytic approach is something Ayer was not in fact guilty of—relativism. Again, there is a factual relativism that is beyond dispute—people do indeed, in different societies and different cultures, at different times and in different places, have differing conceptions of what is right and wrong, good and bad. But this does not place these competing views on a level footing. The element of decision that the emotive and subsequent attitudinal analyses of ethics stressed is decision in favour of a particular set of values; and moral choice, once made, automatically excludes its competitors. In other words, there is a firmness of moral commitment built in even to attitudinal analyses of ethics. It is not necessary to find a metaphysical or authoritarian justification of objective values to justify positive commitment on ethical issues.

The ethical aspects of the logical positivist strand of the analytic tradition are not, then, as negative in their implications as they are often thought to be. And since it is not possible to separate the ethical theory from its epistemological roots, this is a conclusion of some significance. Subsequent contributions to ethical theory have tended to offer an ethics or social theory developed in isolation from a broader philosophical position. The emotive theory and its immediate successors offered an approach developed as a consequence of, and in conjunction with, views about logic, meaning, and knowledge. In this respect, it remains in some form or other of continuing interest to the empirically minded.

Notes

The two essays included in this chapter are adapted from papers read in Prague in 1982 at unofficial philosophy seminars that were part of a course on analytic philosophy given by academic "visitors" from England.

G. E. MOORE

1. G. E. Moore, "A Defence of Common Sense," in *Contemporary British Philosophy*, ed. J. H. Muirhead, 2nd ser., 1925, reprinted in *Philosophical Papers* (London: Allen & Unwin, 1959). See full critical discussions of this paper by Norman Malcolm, "Defending Common Sense," *The Philosophical Review* 58 (1949): 201–20 and in A. J. Ayer, *Russell and Moore: the Analytic Heritage* (London: Macmillan, 1971), chap. 7.
2. B. Russell, "My Mental Development," in *The Philosophy of Bertrand Russell*, ed. P. A. Schilpp, (New York: Harper & Row, 1963), p. 12.
3. J. M. Keynes, *Two Memoirs* (London: Rupert Hart Davies, 1949), p. 94.
4. Letter from Lytton Strachey to Moore, 11 October 1903, printed in Paul Levy, *Moore* (London: Weidenfeld & Nicolson, 1979), p. 234.
5. G. E. Moore, "The Refutation of Idealism," *Mind*, n.s., 12 (1903), reprinted in G. E. Moore, *Philosophical Studies* (London: Routledge & Kegan Paul, 1960), pp. 1–30.
6. On the relation between Moore's epistemological and ethical views, see also R. Bambrough, *Moral Scepticism and Moral Knowledge* (London, Routledge & Kegan Paul, 1979), chap. 2.
7. R. M. Hare, *The Language of Morals* (Oxford: Oxford University Press, 1952).
8. These questions are ably discussed by R. F. Tredwell in "On Moore's Analysis of Goodness," *The Journal of Philosophy* 59 (1962): 793–802, reprinted in E. D. Klemke, *Studies in the Philosophy of G. E. Moore* (Chicago: Quadrangle, 1969), pp. 53–63.
9. The argument is presented in G. E. Moore, *Principia Ethica* (Cambridge: Cambridge University Press, 1903), chap. 1.
10. See W. K. Frankena, "The Naturalistic Fallacy," *Mind* 48 (1939), reprinted in W. Sellars and J. Hospers, *Readings in Ethical Theory* (New York: Appleton-Century-Crofts, 1952), pp. 103–14.
11. See G. A. Paul, "G. E. Moore: Analysis, Common Usage and Common Sense," in A. J. Ayer et al., *The Revolution in Philosophy* (London: Macmillan, 1956).
12. The utilitarian aspect of Moore's thought is more clearly exemplified in his *Ethics* (1912; reprint, London: Oxford University Press, 1947).
13. G. Warnock, *Contemporary Moral Philosophy* (London: Macmillan, 1967). See, however,

Moore's own reply to his critics in P. A. Schilpp, ed., *The Philosophy of G. E. Moore*, 2nd ed. (New York: Tudor, 1952), pp. 535–611.
14. Moore, *Principia Ethica* (1903; reprint, New York: Cambridge University Press, 1959), chap. 6.

A. J. AYER

15. A. J. Ayer, *Language, Truth and Logic* 2nd ed. (London: Gollancz, 1946), pp. 102–3.
16. Quoted in A. J. Ayer, *Part of my Life* (London: Oxford University Press, 1978), p. 54.
17. D. Hume, *An Enquiry Concerning Human Understanding*, sec. 12, p. 3 ed. L. A. Selby-Bigge (Oxford Clarendon Press, 1955), p. 165.
18. L. Wittgenstein, *Tractatus Logico-Philosophicus* 1921; reprint, (London: Routledge & Kegan Paul, 1961), p. 21 (proposition 4.024).
19. For discussion of the verification principle, see M. Schlick, "Meaning and Verification," *Philosophical Review* (1936), reprinted in H. Feigl and W. Sellars, *Readings in Philosophical Analysis* (New York: Appleton-Century-Crofts, 1949), pp. 146–70; J. Passmore, *Philosophical Reasoning* (London: Duckworth, 1961), pp. 81–99; C. G. Hempel, "Problems and Changes in the Empiricist Criterion of Meaning," *Review Internationale de Philosophie* (1950), reprinted in *Logical Positivism*, ed. A. J. Ayer (Urbana: University of Illinois Press, 1959); F. Waismann, *How I See Philosophy* (London: Macmillan, 1968), chap. 2 "Verifiability."

Ayer succinctly explained the consequences of the verification principle for ethics in the following terms: "Leaving metaphysics aside, there were two important kinds of statements which the acceptance of the verification principle made it difficult to treat as statements of fact: the *a priori* statements of logic and pure mathematics, and statements of value, whether moral or aesthetic" (A. J. Ayer et al., *The Revolution in Philosophy* [London: Macmillan, 1956]).

20. Ayer, *Language, Truth and Logic*, p. 107.
21. Ibid., p. 108.
22. C. K. Ogden, and I. A. Richards, *The Meaning of Meaning*: (1923).
23. C. D. Broad, "Is 'Goodness' the Name of a Simple Non-Natural Quality?" *Proceedings of the Aristotelian Society*, 1933–4.
24. A. Hägerstrom, "On the Truth of Moral Propositions," in *Philosophy and Religion* (London: Allen & Unwin, 1964), p. 92.
25. C. L. Stevenson, *Ethics and Language* (New Haven: Yale University Press, 1944). The theory is discussed with special reference to Stevenson in J. O. Urmson, *The Emotive Theory of Ethics* (London: Hutchinson, 1968).
26. This seems to echo a passage in Hume's *Treatise of Human Nature*, bk 3, p. 1, sec 1, ed. L. A. Selby-Bigge 1952 (Oxford: Oxford University Press, 1952), p. 468.
27. A. J. Ayer, "On the Analysis of Moral Judgements," in *Philosophical Essays*, (London: Macmillan, 1954), p. 242.
28. Ibid., pp. 237–38.
29. A. J. Ayer, "Man as a Subject for Science," in *Metaphysics and Common Sense* (London: Macmillan, 1967), pp. 219–39.
30. A. J. Ayer, "Freedom and Necessity," in *Philosophical Essays*, pp. 271–84.
31. A. J. Ayer, "Philosophy and Politics," in *Metaphysics and Common Sense*, pp. 240–60.

9
An Ethical Paradox

"Everyone ought to do what he thinks he ought to do."

People who are tolerant of ethical views that differ from their own, and who are undogmatic about the moral views they themselves hold, often express, as one of their own moral views, a principle equivalent to the one quoted above, which I shall call therefore the principle of moral nondogmatism. The element of repetition in the principle as written above may prevent it often being uttered in precisely those words, although it sometimes is; but it is recognisable under several light disguises. The same judgement is expressed, for instance, when someone says, "People ought to do what they conceive to be their duty," and acceptance of it is, perhaps less obviously, implied when people say in mitigation, "He honestly thought it was the only right thing to do," or "People can only act according to their light." This last statement implies that it is unreasonable to expect a person to act according to the speaker's moral principles if these are not his own, either because the society he lives in has not reached the same degree of civilisation, or because, while living in a civilised society, he has not had the benefit of an adequate standard of education.

This way of thinking has very respectable philosophical backing. Indeed it is entailed by a principle that has gained almost universal acceptance among moral philosophers, the Kantian principle, that is, that "ought" implies "can." For to ask a person to behave morally is to ask that he should consider what is right or wrong in a particular case, and whether any action is morally obligatory or not. It is to ask also that, having decided what he ought to do, he should "set himself" to do it. More than this he cannot do. To add a demand that he should make sure that the moral decisions he makes are the right ones is not to plot out for him any further course of action; it is in fact comparable to saying that people should verify whether those propositions they have carefully decided are true, really are true. Unless this is a demand for some new investigations not already undertaken, or for a repeat of those already completed, it is a demand for the impossible, that is, that someone should step outside his own frame of reference, know what he is not in a position to know, judge what he is not in a position to judge. But according to Kant's principle, it can never be a person's duty to do what he cannot do. It seems to follow, then, that it can only be his duty to do what he thinks he ought to do, as opposed to what he "really" ought to do. Plausible as this sounds, however, its acceptance generates a series of ethical paradoxes similar to those that arise in logic when self-reference is combined with certain types of predicate, notably "true" and "false." But this is not a semantic paradox; there is in fact no self-reference, and the notions of truth and falsity are not directly involved. So these paradoxes cannot be dismissed by, for instance, an ethical Theory of Types; they go deeper than meanings of words, and their acceptance could involve, for those who have held the principle that gives rise to them, a fundamental change in moral attitude.

The first paradoxical consequence of the principle of moral nondogmatism arises from the fact that it is a principle of toleration, and as a principle of toleration, leads to the general dilemma of toleration: that the toleration of intolerance is self-destructive. It is recognition of this fact that has led, in the political sphere, to a limitation on laws allowing freedom of opinion and speech, according to which freedom to advocate the overthrow of the system involving toleration of opinion is sometimes not allowed, and almost invariably the advocacy of the forceful or unconstitutional overthrow of the system is not allowed. Similarly, in the ethical sphere, a principle like the principle of moral nondogmatism would also be self-destructive, would cancel itself out, unless some restriction were specified in cases in which what some people conceived to be their duty was to prevent other people from doing what they conceived to be their duty. As an example one could take a hypothetical case in the days of the Inquisition, in which the heretic being burned held his heresy on principle, and also believed the propagation of the heresy to be his duty. Here, holding that what the Inquisitors ought to do is to follow their own conception of their duty, is to deny this same possibility to the heretic.

However, apart from this self-defeating tendency of the principle when held without qualification, there are some consequences of an equally paradoxical nature that follow for even a qualified profession of a principle of this sort, and these are what I want here to discuss.

Where someone puts forward a principle of nondogmatism in morals, he may be under the impression that what he is putting forward is a moral view of a unique kind, and one that supersedes all the moral principles of a more specific kind that he personally holds. For instance, a person holding such a principle may say to someone else: "I think lying is wrong; however, yours is the decision (to lie or not to lie) in this particular case, and as long as you do what after honest deliberation you think you ought to do—if you, for instance, decide that you ought to tell a lie—then I shall not condemn you; on the contrary, I shall think you have acted rightly."

Plausible as this seems, however, there are considerations that may convince the person expressing this seemingly unexceptionably reasonable viewpoint that the principle he is expressing has no such unique status, but is simply one among the various moral principles that he holds, some more strongly than others, some less strongly. Nor, if moral principles are conceived of as occupying a scale according to their degree of strength, would nondogmatism be distinguished by appearing at either end of the scale, as either the most significant or the least significant of moral principles.

One can only use an *ad hominem* argument here, and appeal to what it seems that almost anyone would accept; but it would seem that there are in fact some moral principles that are held with such intensity that they would by general acknowledgement supersede the principle of moral nondogmatism. One such more powerful principle would be:

P. One ought not to organise or set about committing genocide.

Trials of Nazi war criminals suggest that in a case as ultimate as this, the fact that it is sincerely believed to be a duty is not considered actually to make genocide a duty, neither is it even accepted as a mitigating factor. There are, of course, other legal examples; to have thought it one's duty to commit murder or theft would not be accepted in mitigation, either. However, the law is bound to be specific; morality is not. Morally, one might not condemn the man who murders or robs because he thinks it right; for example, the political assassin in some circumstances might be respected, as is the memory of Robin Hood's socialistic robberies. But in the example I have suggested, of genocide, there appears to be no difference of viewpoint between the findings of the law and the findings of moral opinion. What is legally not an excuse or justification is not morally an excuse or justification either.

This suggests, then, that where an action generates a really high degree of moral abhorrence, the principle of respect for other people's moral views fades into insignificance. It is only consideration of less strongly held moral views as examples that leads some morally tolerant people to attach special significance to the principle of moral nondogmatism, and to suppose that it takes precedence over any other moral view. Two examples are sufficient to show how nondogmatism may seem to have more significance than it in fact has: pacifism, and sexual promiscuity.

Two principles could be formulated:
Q. People ought to fight to defend their country, and
R. People ought not to be sexually promiscuous.

Where a person or a society holding either of these views holds them with less strength than the principle of moral nondogmatism, then the person or the society is willing, in spite of its disapproval, to tolerate pacifism and sexual promiscuity. There may, of course, be other reasons for tolerating them, and I am not here even raising the question of whether they are right or wrong, good or bad. This is simply an argument to show that where all three moral views are held—nondogmatism, and the propositions Q and R, then very often nondogmatism is held to take precedence as a moral principle over the other two.[1]

But it is precisely at this point that the paradox of nondogmatism appears. The paradox is as follows:

If one holds that people ought to do what they think they ought to do, and if there are in fact pacifists, that is, people who believe they ought not to fight and also people who are morally opposed to the conventional views on sexual morality to the extent of advocating sexual promiscuity, then it would seem that the moral nondogmatist, whether a society or an individual, is committed to holding that, for these two groups of people, it is the case that they ought respectively, not to fight for their country, and ought to be sexually promiscuous. This is to say that, for the nondogmatist, it seems to follow that it would actually be wrong for a person who believed in promiscuity not to be sexually promiscuous, as it would be for a convinced pacifist to fight. But whereas it may seem reasonable to tolerate practices in others that run counter to one's own moral views, it seems very much less reasonable to hold a principle that not merely permits but demands behaviour that, according to other moral notions of the holder of the principle, is wrong. It is so far from reasonable, in fact, that the principle of moral nondogmatism may be seen to earn the epithet *paradoxical* by involving its holder in contradiction: the hypothetical holder in this case holds first and directly that people ought to fight to defend their country, but via the principle, that people ought not to fight to defend their country; and again he holds directly and for its own sake that promiscuity is wrong, but, via the principle, that promiscuity is morally obligatory.

Before going on to discuss one of these examples in more detail, it may be advisable to summarise this argument. Briefly it is this: that whereas it seems immediately possible to hold the principle of moral nondogmatism in conjunction with principles like Q and R, and many liberal-minded people may claim to do this, there is nevertheless something logically odd about this combination. Further, that there are some principles like P, in conjunction with which only an extremist could think of holding the principle of nondogmatism.

At this point, I should like to deal with a possible objection. It may be argued that if someone disagrees with the assertion that "One ought to do x," this may be because he holds either (1) "It is not the case that one ought to do x" or (2) "One ought not to do x." The former is the contradiction of the original assertion; the latter the contrary. And it might seem that my argument fails to take account of the first kind of disagreement, which indeed might be thought to express the nondogmatic position on any issue most accurately. For instance, one might deny the assertion "One ought to go to church on Sundays" by making the totally neutral assertion that "It is not wrong to go, and it is not wrong not to go." This is to say, in fact, that instead of countering the assertion, "One ought to do x," with a rival moral assertion, one may counter it instead with a denial that the issue is a moral one. However, my argument is not intended to suggest that there is anything either odd or paradoxical about a position of moral neutrality, and therefore, I would concede that a denial of "One ought to go to church on Sundays" need not take the form "One ought not to go to church on Sundays." My point applies only where a moral attitude is in fact already adopted, and in these cases, I am suggesting, one cannot sit on both sides of the fence at once. Where one already has a moral viewpoint, one cannot without contradiction, allow that opposed moral viewpoints may have equal validity.

But this may become clearer from more detailed examination of the examples. Of these, pacifism is perhaps the more interesting case, for many people do as a matter of fact imagine that it is possible to hold an open (i.e., a nondogmatic) position on this subject. For example, A. MacIntyre, in a paper entitled "What Morality is Not," represents a pacifist as saying, "I ought to abstain from participation in war, but I cannot criticise or condemn responsible nonpacifists."[2] MacIntyre sees this as meaning that the nondogmatic pacifist believes that he himself ought not to fight, whereas other people, who are not pacifists, ought in fact to fight. In MacIntyre's paper, this view is put forward against Hare's principle of universalizability, which can perhaps most succinctly be described as the view that "I ought to do x" entails "One ought to do x." More fully, it is the view that if anyone sincerely believes that some course of action is his duty in a particular set of circumstances, then he must, logically, believe that anyone else, who is not dissimilar to him in any ethically relevant respect, has the same duty in any similar set of circumstances. This is put forward as a logical view because Hare holds universalizability to be a defining feature of the moral, as opposed to practical, hortatory, etc., uses of *ought*.

MacIntyre, on the other hand, introduces the example of the person I have called the nondogmatic pacifist, together with several others—Captain Oates, for instance, and duties of supererogation—to show that it is possible to have an entirely personal duty, that in no way implies a universal one.

It will be seen that if this view of MacIntyre's is correct, the view that is to say, which, following Gellner, came to be characterised as existentialist, then indeed there is nothing logically odd about holding that some people ought to fight, others ought not, although there is no distinction between them other than one of moral attitude.[3] It follows, then, that the logical untenability of nondogmatism in morals is closely associated with the logical necessity, or analyticity, of universalizability. What the universalizability principle denies is that there can be private moral duties; what the principle of nondogmatism asserts, *inter alia*, is that there can.

Much depends then, on the counterexamples that have been adduced to show that universalizability does not have the all-embracing status of a necessary truth.

One of these counterexamples has already been mentioned: the nondogmatic pacifist whose point of view has been summed up by MacIntyre. Against this, I would like to suggest that one might consider the position of such a pacifist before a Conscientious Objectors' tribunal. Such tribunals were conducted on an extremely rigorous basis, and if a would-be conscientious objector had tried to maintain that just he, and nobody else, ought to abstain from fighting, then he would, I suggest, have had very little chance of establishing, to the judges' satisfaction, that he was a genuine, fully-committed pacifist or conscientious objector. For, to be a pacifist in a sense that would have satisfied a legally recognised tribunal meant convincing the tribunal of one's conviction that fighting (or killing) was wrong; and the assertion that it is wrong in this strong moral sense involves the assertion that it is wrong for anyone to fight and not just wrong for a few selected individuals whose minds run in a particular way. What MacIntyre's pacifist is really doing is taking up the position toward nonpacifists that an advanced and highly civilised society is prepared to take up toward its pacifists: whereas society dissociates itself from the moral viewpoint of the pacifist, and indeed holds strongly that people ought to fight to defend their country, it is prepared to allow a tiny proportion of people of different views to act in accordance with their own principles; there is emphatically no suggestion that society shares in these principles to any degree whatsoever; what society is saying, simply, is that it will not molest or punish those who hold the minority view; neither will it use its powers to force them to conform. Similarly, what MacIntyre's pacifist is really saying is that while not sharing the moral views of the nonpacifist, he will not use such powers as he has (of social ostracism, repeated argument, etc.) to make the holding of the opposite viewpoint unpleasant. He is also making a well-established distinction between the act that the nonpacifist does, and the motive from which it is done, or, if you like, between the nature of the act, and the character of the agent. What he is not committed to is in any way concurring with the moral view that to fight for one's country is right.

This is not to deny, of course, that it may in fact be possible to find pacifists who see no inconsistency in asserting both that they ought not to participate in war, and that others should, although I would suggest that in general this is a mis-description of what they are trying to assert. However, where it is not a mis-description, and this assertion is in fact intended, then this is still no argument for its logical validity. For it is an observable fact that people can both utter and firmly believe logical contradictions. Most obviously they can do this when dealing with advanced mathematics or symbolic logic; but it also happens in everyday life, in both morals and general semiscientific reasoning.

But perhaps it may be thought that there is another way of rationally justifying a belief such as that "*I* ought to abstain from participation in war; others ought not." This is by considering pacifism to be a duty of supererogation. And since duties of supererogation are thought to be a second class of counterexamples to the universalizability thesis, this way out deserves further consideration. I should like to quote what MacIntyre says about duties of supererogation in the article already mentioned:

> A work of supererogation is by definition not numbered among the normal duties of life. . . . A moral hero, such as Captain Oates, is one

> who does more than duty demands. In the universalisable sense of "ought" it does not therefore make sense to assert that Captain Oates did what he ought to have done. To say of a man that he did his duty in performing a work of supererogation is to contradict oneself. Yet a man may set himself the task of performing a work of supererogation and commit himself to it so that he will blame himself if he fails without finding such failure in the case of others blameworthy. Such a man might legitimately say, "I have taken so-and-so as what I ought to do," and here his valuation cannot, logically cannot, be universalised.[4]

The pacifist, then, in restricting his moral judgement to himself, may be saying that he has set himself a higher moral standard than others, one that he will be at fault in not attaining, whereas others, for whom lower standards apply, will have done their duty, albeit at a lower level, in fighting. Similarly, MacIntyre seems to be suggesting, Captain Oates did his duty in relieving his companions of their burden by going away to die, where others would not have failed in their duty in remaining alive. But perhaps it would after all be possible to describe Captain Oates's act of moral heroism, not as an example of a special act of purely personal duty, but either as an act that is in no sense an act of duty at all, or as an ordinary, that is, universalisable, act of duty. In the first case, if saying that Captain Oates did what he ought to have done is the same as saying that what he did was his duty, then it follows that Captain Oates did not do what he ought to have done. Instead, what he did could be classed as some sort of gratuitous act—one that he need not have performed, and would have been no more blameworthy for not having performed, even though he was the person that he was. That the act was gratuitous, rather than obligatory, according to this hypothesis, does not make it, of course, any the less admirable.

It is not impossible, however, to adopt the second approach, and regard Captain Oates's action as an act of duty in the universalisable sense. For it must be allowed that there are duties that is very difficult to perform: for instance, for a Resistance fighter during the war, the duty of not giving away the names of other Resistance fighters under torture. The fact that many people were unable to fulfil this difficult demand did not mean that they were doing their (lesser) duty in betraying their friends. Similarly, although many people would not have Captain Oates's strength of mind, yet it is arguable that in this situation, which must in its essential elements have been repeated many times in, for example, battle conditions, it is the duty of a gravely wounded or ill man to give his comrades a chance of escape by hastening his own end, and so freeing them to save themselves.

There are, of course, moral arguments for and against the view that this is what a person ought to do in such a situation. But the point, I think, has now been established, that it is quite unnecessary to resort to the view that there can be purely personal moral duties in order to account for such examples as Captain Oates's moral heroism.

This is not to deny, however, that there are certain groups of people who may have different (and, depending on one's point of view, higher) obligations than others. For instance, it may be held that a monk has a duty not to marry, or to go barefoot, whereas the ordinary person has no such duties; again, to return to the previous example, a pacifist may also be a Quaker, and it may be thought that a Quaker has a duty to refrain from participation in war, whereas the non-Quaker has not. But these are not genuine counterexamples to the universalizability thesis. On the contrary, they support it. For the duties of the monk or the Quaker are not personal in the sense required, a fact that becomes clear when the principles involved are fully stated. They are (a) that if anyone is a monk, then he ought not to marry, or ought to go barefoot, and of anyone it is then true that if he is a monk, he has failed in his duty if he has violated either of these rules; and (b) that if anyone is a Quaker, then he ought to refrain from participation in war, and again it is true of anyone, that is, universally, that if he is a Quaker, he has failed in his duty if he has not refrained from participation in war. It follows, then, that hypothetical "duties of supererogation" cannot be used as counterexamples to the principle of universalizability. Hence the case for purely personal nonuniversalisable duties is not helped by accounting for the view expressed by the nondogmatic pacifist in terms of duties of supererogation.

One other example that has been used against the principle of universalizability deserves mention, and that is the now famous example of a pupil of J. P. Sartre who, during the war, was faced with two alternatives: either to stay with his dependent mother in France, or to leave her and go to England and join the Free French forces. It is argued here that whichever choice is made, an entirely personal moral decision will have occurred, and hence that it will not be possible, on the basis of this choice, to make a universal judgement of the form "All similar persons in similar circumstances ought to do x."

Against this I would argue, briefly, that if there is genuinely nothing morally to choose between either course of action (let us call the alternative courses of action A and B), then the decision between them is indeed a personal one, but it is not a moral decision, any more than the decision between two tortuous but equally long paths to the same point is a rational one. However, just as there may be scope for a good deal of measurement and calculation in deciding that the two tortuous paths *are* equally long, so there may be much moral reflection and argument leading up to the realisation that morally there is nothing to choose as between course A and course B. In the case of Sartre's pupil, it would no doubt be an exacting moral exercise to decide whether the moral attributes of A exactly counterbalance those of B, and whether the moral omissions involved in B can be set against the moral omissions involved in A. However, if it is decided that this is indeed the case, then the decision between A and B cannot be made on moral grounds; it *must* be a matter of personal feeling.

Of course, it is clear that if all his reflection led Sartre's pupil to the conclusion that A and B did not have equal moral weight, but that one or the other was actually morally preferable, then there would be no reason for seeing this case in any way exceptional; and the obvious implication would be that it would be the duty of any similar person similarly placed (unlikely though it might be that anyone should fit that description) to choose the morally preferable course of action.

I conclude, then, that no counterexamples have been found to invalidate the position of universalizability as a logical criterion for distinguishing moral judgements from other types of judgement. There would, then, be no justification for abandoning universalizability simply in order to avoid what I have called the paradox of nondogmatism. The paradox, then, stands, and provides an argument for the logical inevitability of dogmatism in morals. It becomes necessary to accept as a substitute for the proposition, "Everyone ought to do what he thinks he ought to do," the proposition, "Everyone ought to do what *I* think he ought to do," and to recognise that this substitution embodies the essence of holding a moral opinion. Liberals may reflect, however, that this recognition is itself a greater asset to the cause of toleration than the more sophisticated, but logically untenable, principle of nondogmatism.

Notes

Reprinted from *Mind* 76 (1967): 250–59, by permission of the editor and publishers.
1. The use of the term *proposition* is loose here, and seeks to avoid as here irrelevant the question of the analysis of moral terms, and of whether sentences containing moral words can correctly be held to express propositions.
2. A. MacIntyre, "What Morality is Not," *Philosophy* 32 (1957): pp. 325–35.
3. E. A. Gellner, "Ethics and Logic," *Proceedings of the Aristotelian Society* 55 (1954–55).
4. MacIntyre, "What Morality is Not," p. 328.

10
Three Ethical Fallacies

The aim of establishing systems of ethics on the basis of logic has long been abandoned as a project for moral philosophy. Practical conclusions about what to do, it is generally agreed, cannot be arrived at by mere armchair calculation—they are the prerogative of participating agents operating within a context of practical situations, consequences, and other interacting agents. Nevertheless, while logic may be unable to delimit a positive path, it may yet be of use, it will be argued here, in providing negative guidance by indicating certain pitfalls or logical incoherences that can distort a person's approach to morality—particularly if that person sees himself as adopting a liberal stance on matters of morality.

Three fallacies in particular stand out as currently popular views—views that have been adopted in popular as well as philosophical reasoning—and that, in their acceptance, undermine the moral position of the individual who allows himself to be influenced by them. The term *fallacy* is one that may be much abused, particularly in relation to ethical reasoning, but it will be used here in the informal sense in which inadequate reasoning leading to incorrect conclusions may be called fallacious, rather than in the formal sense in which some kind of error of syllogistic reasoning is detected. The three fallacies, then, that are to be investigated here are, respectively: first, a fallacy connected with individualism; secondly, a fallacy connected with relativism; and thirdly, a fallacy that I should like to call a fallacy of false liberalism. It will be argued that, while clearly being linked with each other, both in the sense that consideration of one leads naturally to consideration of another, and also in the sense that all are fallacies generated by a liberal approach to morality, these are separate and essentially independent ethical fallacies, and each will therefore be considered separately.

The Individualist Fallacy

One of the defendants at the Manson murder trial in California is reported to have said, "What I did was right for me." This statement is interesting in a number of ways. First, it is surprising to find morality invoked at all in connection with a peculiarly brutal multiple murder. But secondly, the concept of morality implied is itself an unusual one. It represents the most extreme form that subjectivism can take—a concept of right that is of singular application only, restricted only to the individual and relevant only to a particular occasion and instance. Nevertheless, it is distinguishable from (although it may be close to) a complete repudiation of morality and a decision simply to please oneself about one's actions, in that a clear imperative element is also implied. Having decided on this very particular and individual right or obligation, it is obviously felt both that it is as binding as more conventionally accepted moral dictates, and also that to some extent at least it can be used as a defence for action taken in order to comply with this intuited individual morality.

If this were an isolated case of the adoption of what might be called a private morality as a determinant of action, then perhaps one might be justified in regarding it as the aberration of a small group of individuals who have never felt the need to subject their concept of morality to the searching light of logical analysis. But if we can bring ourselves to step back from our contemporary scene and see ourselves for a moment as some future historian might see us, then it may well be that, on the contrary, this is the new and distinctive viewpoint of our generation. Its not always conscious similarity to European existentialism, together with its relation to the widespread youth ideal expressed in the slogan "doing one's thing," make of this concept of morality something much more generally accepted than the professional discussions of philosophers would lead one to suppose. Nevertheless, it must be said that a basic logical inconsistency lies at the root of this way of thinking, and while a mere cult of irrationality devoid of all reference to moral obligation is invulnerable to logical attack, there are strong arguments to show that morality, having essential logical characteristics, cannot be conjoined with this cult except by misunderstanding. Indeed it may be argued that the very idea of a private, unique-instance morality is self-contradictory and incoherent; that a moral claim must have *some* wider reference than the individual and the moment, either in the sense that what is claimed about oneself must be taken to apply to others too (must, in other words, be generalisable or universalisable) or at least in the sense that it is of general application to potential future situations in the individual's own life.

Nevertheless, although this form of association may be most strikingly associated with esoteric cults such as the Manson "family," it is also at the same time arguably much more central to Western thought than these particular associations would imply. In the notion of the sacrosanct status of the dictates of individual conscience, another and more generally accepted version of ethical individualism may be found.

The fallacy that lies at the root of such reasoning, however, is the fallacy of confusing two distinct and very different notions:

1. The view that the dictates of the individual conscience are always right, and
2. The view that no individual should be forced to act against the dictates of conscience.

These become conflated in:

3. The view that what a man's conscience dictates is *for him*, always right, with the corollary that it is morally wrong to act against conscience.

But View 1, once stated, can be seen to be inherently self-contradictory, in that it implies that a range of mutually incompatible propositions must all be judged to be right. In the case of ethical propositions, moreover, to assert that they are right is to endorse them. And to endorse simultaneously a range of mutually incompatible statements is to engage in an incoherent and self-nullifying procedure. View 1, then, is logically incoherent and unlikely to be intentionally adopted by anyone who has a clear understanding of what holding it involves.

View 2, on the other hand, is not logically incoherent, nor is there any *a priori* reason why it should not be held by a considerable number of people, whatever their other moral convictions. It is, however, a practical and political principle—a ground-level moral principle—rather than a meta-ethical assertion about the meaning of "*right*" or the nature of duty, or the ultimate ground of moral obligation. Nevertheless, even as a practical principle, it is unlikely to be held in an absolute sense, or without any qualification. While it will be admitted that only with extreme reluctance should anyone (and usually this will mean the state) force anyone else to act against their own conscience, it will, on the whole, tend to be held that this must in the last resort depend upon what an individual's conscience dictates to him. If, for instance, the Moors murderers, Ian Bradley and Myra Hindley, had claimed that for them the ritual torture and murder of young children was a matter of conscience (and they did indeed have some philosophical background to their activities) would this have been a reason for noninterference on the part of others? If it seems unlikely that a conscientious justification would be offered of this nature, then it may be pointed out that as a matter of fact many wartime atrocities that are at least comparable in terms of suffering caused, are indeed defended by those responsible on the basis of a conscientious obligation to obey without question the orders of superior officers.

Even the practical principle expressed by View 2, then, is not without difficulty. The important point, however, is that both it, and View 1, are entirely distinct both from each other and from View 3, with which they may be jointly confused.

View 3, then, which is the view that what a man's conscience dictates is for him always right, derives its plausibility from its resemblance to Views 1 and 2. The addition of "for him," however, which is what distinguishes View 3 from View 1, is strictly meaningless—there is no clear way in which such a phrase can be understood. It cannot, therefore, entail such a proposition as that it is always morally wrong to act against conscience, and while the example of the Nuremberg trials could be held to show that there is a widely accepted view that conscience must be supreme, they can equally and more correctly be taken to show that following one's own view of conscience (that, for a soldier, obedience is the highest value) does not exonerate one from moral responsibility or exempt one from moral condemnation.

A totally personal and individualistic ethic, then, is inevitably grounded on the shifting sands of some version of the individualist fallacy as described here. Moral judgement has, built into its form and structure, a breadth of application that cannot be avoided by extreme versions of even conscientious individualism, and certainly not by the instinct-guided or idiosyncratic individualism implied in the phrase "Right for me."

The Relativist Fallacy

The Relativist Fallacy is the fallacy of supposing that the existence of different moral codes in different societies and in different subgroups within a given society, together with an understanding of the psychological and sociological reasons accounting for these beliefs and variations on them, provides a reason for reducing the commitment one feels to one's own ethical beliefs. At least it may be thought that the existence of other beliefs provides a reason for holding one's own beliefs with less conviction, or for being more ready to make exceptions to the moral rules one has chosen to recognise. But to state this assumption is to see that the existence of alternative codes is strictly irrelevant to the degree of commitment that may be due to one's own.

Sir Isaiah Berlin quoted "an admirable writer of our time," who well summed up the point I am trying to make here: "To realise the relative validity of one's convictions," this writer is reported to have said, "and yet stand for them unflinchingly, is what distinguishes a civilized man from a barbarian."[1] To suppose otherwise is, in effect, to imply a version of the discredited ethical theory that majority opinion defines rightness, or that in the absence of universal consensus, nothing can be held to be right, or that any view is equally right. But such a view could be held only by an external observer, operating from outside the human framework altogether—someone who is not himself a part of the world of which he judges that all views are equal. But of course, no one can possess this detachment, for we are all human beings operating in a world of human beings.

To some extent, such reasoning is based on a false antithesis: either moral values are objective, in which case they will be recognised by a special human faculty most usually characterised as intuition; in this case, no significant differences of moral opinion will be found to exist between honest and serious people who are at an equally advanced stage of development (itself a concept carrying its own set of difficulties); or, alternatively, moral values are subjective, there is no special way of arriving at them, and variations will be found in ethical practice and belief. The first case is thought to justify the strong holding of categorical beliefs and opinions, since I may hold that everyone who disagrees with me is wrong. The second is thought to entail that one should be extremely tentative in holding any moral opinion because anyone who disagrees with those opinions may be right.

Plainly, however, this is not what the subjective/objective dichotomy entails. For if moral values were objective, I would not be entitled to any particular degree of conviction as to the validity of my own particular beliefs, or even those of my social group or my society. The possibility of mistake must still loom large within an objectivist system. Conversely, if moral values are subjective, the mere fact that a belief is a belief of mine entails that it is one I do in fact hold. If I do not hold it with conviction, then it is simply not a particularly strong belief of mine, and only erroneous epistemological considerations could persuade me to put a whole category of beliefs into this limbo of doubtfulness.

It is a weakness of the sociology of knowledge that it starts up an elusive will-o'-the-wisp—a chain of what might be called meta-considerations. Not only ethics, but science, religion, and philosophy are explained and relativised, and from the shifting sands of ordinary forms of knowledge, those who have been persuaded to adopt the sociological perspective attempt to scramble to the firm ground of sociology itself—only to find, of course, that it is as relative as the sciences it appears to supersede. Neither recognition of variation in beliefs, then, nor recognition of the psychosocial origins of belief provide a ground for relativism in any sense that implies equality between one's own beliefs and those of others. Conviction is as appropriate for the anthropologist as for the intuitionist.

The Fallacy of False Liberalism

The Fallacy of False Liberalism is the fallacy of supposing that a liberal position in morality involves holding that everything is permitted. The Relativist Fallacy involved, by contrast, the view that everything is right, and the Individualist Fallacy that rightness is internal to the standards of the individual.

Liberalism, however, is especially associated with toleration, and it may be thought that it involves the lesser commitment of, while not *endorsing* every moral view, at least *permitting* the existence of all moral views as well as their practical expression in behaviour and action, subject to certain well-understood safeguards. In order to make it clear that it is *moral* liberalism that is in question here, rather than the political version of liberalism, something must be said about the way in which *permission* is to be understood.

To begin with, it must be said that permitting people to act on their beliefs is a very different matter from permitting them to hold those beliefs, but given some stipulation about the necessity of allowing conscience a privileged position in determining action, the two may seem inextricably linked. The need to distinguish between action and belief has already been argued, however, in connection with the Individualist Fallacy. In this case, moreover, it is even more clear that action and belief must be treated separately. False liberalism appears to imply that no sanctions should be applied where any moral issue arises. The need to apply sanctions enforcing certain patterns of behaviour in matters in which other people's interests are concerned may be accepted, but then set on one side as coming within the category of politics and social organisation rather than of pure morality. In order to see the issue purely as a moral issue, it is necessary to assume, for the moment, that there is an area of purely self-regarding actions—moral matters whose outcome is of no reasonable interest to anyone other than the individual concerned.

The possible extent of such an area might, for illustrative purposes, be taken to include some of the areas discussed by Hart and Devlin with special reference to the Wolfenden Report—areas such as censorship, pornography, and sexual behaviour, in which the limits of public, as opposed to private interest, are a matter of controversy.[2] The Wolfenden Report, in advocating the abolition of legal sanctions against prostitution as such, and against homosexual relationships between consenting adults, claimed that there must be an area of morality that is "not the law's business." Plainly, this opens up the question: if there is an area of human activity in which there can be no legitimate public interest, perhaps because it is universally agreed that no consequences affecting other people ensue, would the liberal moralist, as opposed to the liberal legislator or judge, be obliged to say that here, at least, everything is permitted? Is a liberal morality one that says (a) that in this area people are permitted to hold whatever moral view they choose, and (b) that they must be permitted to act on the basis of whatever view they have adopted?

As far as the first of these questions is concerned, a negative answer must be given. For a liberal morality is one that includes certain defined values, and not only the values of freedom and toleration.[3] Those whose proposals conflict with any of these values, and not merely the value of freedom, are not "permitted" to hold their alternative values in a *moral* sense of the term, even though it may be wise that they should be permitted in a legal or political sense to hold them. Once again, the notion of moral permission, as opposed to practical permission, is in effect an endorsement of a contrary viewpoint, and as such, essentially fallacious. The second question, however, is ambiguous: the liberal legislator must allow people to act within this area on whatever view they have formed. The liberal moralist, however, while necessarily following suit, must be careful to avoid having his "permission" interpreted as endorsement.

True as opposed to false liberalism, then, involves holding firmly to a particular set of principles, and, inevitably, in holding these principles, the liberal becomes a proselytiser for his own point of view. He cannot, therefore, give his *moral* permission or endorsement to other positions, even though his espousal of the principle of individual freedom and toleration will entail a higher degree of permissiveness in practice than would be the case if he did not set a high value on these things.

The fallacy of False Liberalism, then, lies in equating practical permission with moral permission, toleration of a moral viewpoint with endorsement of that viewpoint, and the advocacy of freedom with a lack of commitment to any particular moral viewpoint.

The position that exposure of these three fallacies points to could well be called a theory of dogmatic or positive liberalism, and, in conclusion, some of the conclusions implicit in such a position will be indicated.

The Theory of Positive Liberalism

The notion of positive liberalism involves reference to a pluralistic value system that includes some familiar, not to say traditional values (at least in Western culture), and there are other descriptions therefore, that might be equally appropriate. Some Christian ethical viewpoints, for instance, would not differ drastically from the view described here as liberalism, and other religions, too, would possibly be found to have much in common with such a value system. Essentially, however, a secular viewpoint is of wider interest, and while a variety of alternative names might be at least as appropriate—some might prefer, for instance, the term *liberal humanism*—the concept of liberalism does convey a certain well-understood range of values.

But to speak of *positive* liberalism, with the overtones of dogmatism that this conveys, may seem to be unduly paradoxical. Indeed, it may be argued, it is liberalism's essentially nondogmatic nature that has led to the general deterioration in its standing as a reasonable and acceptable approach, and its replacement with firmer, more uncompromising approaches to the problems of society and of personal life. This, however, is precisely the reason for the juxtaposition of the terms: to reject liberal values as a result of recognising the need for firmness and commitment, is to open the door to acceptance of illiberal value systems that, while supplying the firm ground essential for morality, can furnish considerably less nourishment for the human spirit than the system that is being rejected. In seeing firmness of purpose and attitude as an essential aspect of liberalism, the temptation to opt for a totally different value system is so much diminished.

In considering such a liberal system of values, it can be seen that the three fallacies that have been described here are significant insofar as they each tend to affect the degree of conviction with which the liberal will hold to his values, and individually or collectively, they make of liberalism a value system with a permanent tendency to slip into the extreme form of individualism described in relation to the first fallacy. If this tendency can be avoided, through the application of the logical arguments produced here, there is no reason why the values traditionally associated with the term *liberalism* should not be reasserted more forcefully and decisively than ever. These values will be chosen however, not because they seem to represent neutrality, or because they avoid the need for commitment, but simply because in the perennial conflict between the light and the dark, they are judged to represent the former rather than the latter.

The practical consequences of such a view will be seen in a greater unwillingness on the part of those who profess to share liberal values to accommodate opposed viewpoints. If they believe in free speech, for instance, they will not be willing to adopt a position that appears to endorse its suppression. They will appreciate, in an unambiguous way, the inevitability of conflict on fundamental moral matters, and the impossibility, as well as inadvisability, of adopting a stance of sympathetic partial agreement with each and every alternative moral viewpoint. In favouring the plurality of liberal values, they will not feel at a disadvantage when confronted, for instance, with the utilitarian assumption of happiness as the only ultimate value, because they will have recognised that, in the last analysis, no value is supported, defended, or proved—but simply chosen because of its intrinsic nature. Those who recognise only one such value will thus be seen to be in fundamental opposition to those who prefer the plurality of liberal or humanist values, but their case will be based on no firmer ground.

Instead of seeking compromise between his own views and those of others, or between the principles he espouses and the consequences of applying them in particular situations, the liberal who has avoided the fallacies that have been described here will, in his own self-recognition, become a figure of consequence on the moral scene—a figure of some definition, rather than a chameleon, which takes on the colour of whatever object lies nearest at the time of viewing. It is this chameleon characteristic of liberalism that has been most destructive of the standing of the liberal system of values; and it is this concept that, followed through to its conclusion, produces, on the one hand, the aberration of the extreme individualistic ethic summed up in the phrase "Right for me," and on the other hand, the extreme of toleration and neutrality that an ill-defined relativism wrongly appears to entail.

Notes

Reprinted from *Mind* 86 (1977): 78–87, by permission of the editor and publishers.
1. I. Berlin, *Two Concepts of Liberty*, (London: Oxford University Press, 1958), p. 57.
2. H. L. A. Hart, *Law, Liberty and Morality*, (London: Oxford University Press, 1971), and P. Devlin, *The Enforcement of Morals* (London: Oxford University Press, 1965).
3. It would be hard to understand the claim that someone was a liberal, for instance, if humanity and benevolence were not among his values. There would also seem to be a requirement that he should favour truth and openness. On the other hand, justice, fairness, and egalitarianism do not seem to be an essential part of the definition of a (moral) liberal.

11
Positive Values

"Questions of ends are questions of values, and on values reason is silent."[1]

It is this projection of emotivism that forms a central strand in Alasdair MacIntyre's *After Virtue*, and it is an image of emotivism that lends support to the twin assumptions that only an ethical objectivist can engage in a reasoned quest for common human values, and that if radical choice is the root of ethical reflection, there is nothing of importance to be said about morality. These twin assumptions, though, perpetuate certain familiar oppositions in the field of ethics: between relative and absolute values; between cognitive and attitudinal interpretations of moral judgements; between subjectivity and objectivity; between liberal flexibility of moral judgement and belief in fixed, unchanging values. But to be trapped within these particular dichotomies is, I would suggest, to limit the scope for moral action and endeavour both unacceptably and unnecessarily. Instead, I shall argue that there is a third alternative, a notion of positive values, that is more fruitful in its possibilities than either relativism or objectivism, and that incidentally offers a route to moral commitment that is as open to the emotivist who is the subject of MacIntyre's attack as it is to the intuitionist. This *fruitfulness of possibility*—a phrase that encompasses practical utility as well as logical and emotional force—follows from the fact that the notion of positive values retains the force of the epithets *absolute*, *fixed*, and *objective*, but can be freed from the metaphysical overtones that make these notions' unacceptable to the secular-minded empiricist.

For the empiricist, some form of ethical naturalism may seem unavoidable. Where this is so, the strongest appeal may well lie in that form of ethical naturalism that finds an explanation of morality in a single concept such as happiness, since this makes the minimum demand for unargued commitment to principle or value. But to point out even this minimal degree of commitment will be objectionable to ethical naturalists whose position is intended to avoid evaluation altogether. They may say, for example, that their claim is not that human happiness is a goal worth pursuing, but rather that people necessarily pursue happiness; or, if their viewpoint is Marxist rather than utilitarian, that they are not urging the unity of the workers, but simply asserting the inevitability of the victory of the proletariat. But against these claims must be set the difficulty of maintaining this kind of consistency. For moral commitment is only really avoided by psychopaths, and they are not interested in conducting moral arguments. Everyone else adopts a moral stance simply in the process of living and making choices, and this is as true of ethical naturalists as anybody else. Indeed, their interest in theoretical questions of morals may well be occasioned by their practical moral concerns, as the example of Marx and the utilitarians demonstrates.

But ethical naturalism in its different forms is not the only enemy of the notion of positive values. Nor is it the only refuge of the empiricist. On the contrary, the development of various kinds of noncognitive theories of ethics has brought with it an even stronger repudiation of what might be called realist claims about moral values. It has also brought about a consequent renunciation of ethics as a suitable and proper pursuit for philosophers. These remarks of Hans Reichenbach are typical of many similar statements by distinguished exponents of ethics in the present century: "Whoever wants to study ethics . . . should not go to the philosopher; he should go where moral issues are fought out. He should live in the community of a group where life is made vivid by competing volitions, be it the group of a political party, or of a trade union or of a professional organisation, or of a ski club, or a group formed by common study in a classroom."[2]

But the view that philosophers can only help with substantial questions of morals if morals are a matter of fact is surely mistaken. Competing volitions are as legitimate an area for critical analysis and evaluation as anything else. I would suggest, in fact, that what has *really* happened in the present century is not that one conception of morality has replaced another—explanation in terms of reason being displaced by explanation in terms of fact or feeling—but that one set of moral preoccupations has come to seem increasingly irrelevant and trivial. It is the moral examples that philosophers have used that have changed, rather than the nature of the discussion.

Another way to put this is to say that certain traditional interests—truthfulness, fair dealing, sexual restraint, financial probity, reliability in the matter of borrowing and returning books—have been replaced as matters for serious moral concern by others. In other words, disagreement that is on the surface theoretical is at root substantial and practical. Whether the same values are involved is itself an important question, but the problems on which attention is now focused have changed. They fall into two groups: those on a large political and social scale—concerning, for example, war, poverty, injustice, and discrimination—and those in a more intimate and personal dimension—concerning sex and family life, for instance; personal development and self-fulfilment; living by the intellect or living by the mood of the moment. Taken together, these form the macro- and the microquestions of contemporary ethical thinking.

Varying religious and political ideologies provide positions that have ready-made answers to both the new and the old questions for those who subscribe to them. For their adherents, moral problems may be a matter of working out the details rather than of debating the principles. The problem posed by the transformation of moral concerns is a problem, then, not so much for the ideologically committed, as for the more austere thinker whose options are limited by a personal intellectual preference for economy of beliefs. Here ontological assertions about values seem an unwarranted intrusion into the world he has ruthlessly pruned of surplus entities. Philosophical developments in ethics are usually prompted by a need to keep step with developments in epistemology and logic and the pruning of entities that has dominated these areas in the present century has naturally been accompanied by a desire to do the same, using similar tools, in ethics. This desire for economy is well displayed in the following passage from A. J. Ayer's "On the Analysis of Moral Judgements":

> The problem is not that the subjectivist denies that certain wild, or domesticated, animals, "objective values," exist and the objectivist triumphantly produces them; or that the objectivist returns like an explorer with tales from the kingdom of values and the subjectivist says he is a liar. It does not matter what the explorer finds or does not find. For talking about values is not a matter of describing what may or may not be there, the problem being whether it really is there. There is no such problem.[3]

But, in fact, the claim that values exist and the claim that there are no such things as values are both important and significant claims. It was a mistake of some consequence to appear to deny this. That analysis can eliminate the existential form of the assertion is, on the other hand, perfectly correct. The assertion of values is as consistent with attitudinal analyses of ethics as it is with intuitionism. The only difference, after factual argument has run its course, between noncognitivists of many stripes and hues and intuitionists is the opinion of the first that ultimate value judgements are matters of feeling, of commitment or noncommitment, of decision for or decision against, and the opinion of the second that they are better described as a special kind of fact—one that cannot be empirically established.

The denial of values, on the other hand, almost invariably ends up as some form of relativism because, while it is possible to deny that values exist, it is hardly possible to deny that as a matter of fact people do have values—there are moralities, it will be conceded, but it will also be pointed out that these differ from place to place and culture to culture.

Value, though, is a relational concept involving two terms, an object as well as a subject. The ethical objectivist could be said to be focusing exclusively on what is valued—the object—while the ethical subjectivist focuses on the subject, the valuer. If this is so, the elimination of either term of the relation must be an error. In other areas of philosophy it is a commonplace that disputes of the form "Does so and so exist?" are analysable in ways that avoid the tendentious term *exist*, and where there is doubt about the existence of the so and so are better so analysed. But there is a significant asymmetry between eliminating the positive existential claim about values and eliminating the negative claim. While it is harmless, and may be attractive, to translate "values exist" as "something is valuable," the translation of "values do not exist" as "nothing is valuable" suggests not merely relativism but moral nihilism. We should distinguish, therefore, the question of what people mean or intend by the assertion or denial of values from the question of what an analysis of their assertion involves. Analysis need not place values in a special limbo where they must enjoy *sui generis* respect or contempt, with the dice loaded in favour of the latter. The problem about the existence of values is neither greater nor less than the problem about the existence of material objects, or numbers, or classes, or ultimate unobservable particles of matter.

The argument then turns on which is the more productive and constructive: the denial of values, or the assertion of values. Before considering the case for the second, it will be useful to explore some of the disadvantages of the first. These disadvantages follow principally from the uncertainty of evaluation that such a denial produces. The consequences of this uncertainty deserve more attention than they usually receive.

The Cult of the Collective

In *After Virtue*, MacIntyre describes a connection between the loss of a firm basis for evaluation, which he associates with emotivism, and certain kinds of social arrangements, in particular the contemporary phenomenon of *bureaucratic individualism*, a term that in the end it becomes clear is not to be distinguished from *liberal individualism*.[4] MacIntyre explains this concept as a combination of social atomism or *anomie* on the one hand, and manipulative social relationships on the other—Kant combined with utilitarianism. He argues that it leads to a disconnected conception of the self lacking in depth, consistency, and continuity. Indeed, this self, he claims, is the modern self, the "existentialist" self, separated from inherited modes of thought and practice—the individual of emotivist-inspired liberal individualism.

But though this is clearly a subtle and perceptive comment on the contradictions or competing directions present within a contemporary liberal society, it presents a distorted picture of the balance between these two trends. For the denial of values in fact leads most directly to a retreat in the direction of collectivism, rather than to any form of individualism. This is noticeable in the case of various groups committed to the repudiation of objective values, whether on the basis of Marxism or on the basis of some newer form of radicalism. The hallmark of the point of view I have in mind is an ideological attachment to collective decision making, collective action, and collective identity. The notion of hierarchy is so repugnant to this way of thinking that even the pressing of an argument by an individual is regarded as pressing a claim to dominance and superiority. Such groups sometimes actively pursue the elimination of individual identity by using first names only and avoiding the identification of individuals wherever possible. The problem this poses from the moral point of view is that morality is fundamentally an individual matter. The only form of responsibility is individual responsibility. On the other hand, the groups mentioned may actually make much of the notion of collective responsibility when, for example, they hold a race responsible for the oppression of another race, or the male sex responsible for the oppression of the female sex. But there is essentially no tradition of morality that does not involve taking personal responsibility for, and only for, what one has chosen, initiated, and carried through oneself. Mere conformity to social norms is no more than reflex reaction, becoming morality only when it is itself the result of autonomous choice.

So why should the cult of the collective have begun to gain such ground? One answer seems to be that it is associated with a particular and peculiar notion of liberty. Democratic theory, as well as Kant, has accustomed us to the notion that decisions in which we have participated are free decisions, while decisions imposed on us by someone else are unfree. It seems to follow that by collectivising the maximum of decisions we can generate the maximum of liberty. If a group of ten, for instance, has ten decisions to make regarding its activities and each member of the group takes responsibility for one of these decisions, it would seem that their freedom of choice is mathematically limited as compared with a situation in which all ten together make all ten decisions. This looks plausible if, for instance, the group is arranging a conference, or a bazaar, or a concert, and all decisions are talked through and some consensus is sought.

But let us indulge in a typical philosophical ploy and place our ten decision makers on a desert island and let us set them the straightforward tasks of deciding times for breakfast, lunch, and dinner. It is difficult to see in what way their liberty would be enhanced if, instead of each eating when preferred, they attempted to reach agreement as to the ideal times for meals and then ate at those times. Of course, there might be good reasons for setting this up as a collective decision—a preference for eating together, for instance, would be sufficient, or the economy of effort or of fuel secured by joint meals, and so on. But these are practical and nonideological reasons that would justify them all accepting a limitation on their liberty for other gains, while what we are considering is the view that liberty is, in fact, increased by the collective nature of the decision. For there are other decisions they might need to make that would not have any particular practical effects of a mutually affecting nature. What to wear, for example. Whether to pray, or make up poems. Whether to observe the wild life or collect botanical specimens. In practice, human experience has shown that people like to influence each other in these and many other ways. The conduct of others in what does not concern us is of abiding interest.

But by what stretch of the imagination could removing these decisions from the hands of the individual and making them the subject of collective decision enhance liberty? Such control is voluntarily accepted in some religious orders, but it conspicuously involves the surrender of personal autonomy and the renunciation of the will—and again a loss of personal identity with, often, the voluntary taking of a new name. It is indicative of the strength of saints against such pressures and against their own desires that they have, down to Mother Teresa in the present day, made famous or enduring certain simple first names that were originally assumed in order, consciously and explicitly, to abnegate private personality.

Whether consciously or not, it is such ideals that influence present-day secular and sectarian groups whose desire to eliminate the individual is based on some much more tenuous theoretical background. As part of this theoretical background, a reluctance to make a personal and individual claim of an ethical nature is an important determining condition. The burden of individual choice is submerged in the collective will, and the possibility of identification and of challenge on one's beliefs and values is avoided by the merging of personal into collective identity.

The Crisis of Commitment

Reluctance to be associated with a particular moral position need not, of course, be expressed by sheltering behind a collective identity. It can, instead, take the form of a simple avoidance of personal commitment. Within moral philosophy, the avoidance of commitment has become, in effect, a substantial moral position, so much so that it is no exaggeration to speak of a crisis of commitment within the philosophical world. The sharp distinctions philosophers have felt impelled to draw, first, between ethics and other aspects of philosophy, and second, between the moral commitments they are prepared to take on as private persons and the moral commitments they might consider in their capacity as philosophers engaged in moral philosophy, have denied any sense of moral purpose or direction to philosophy within this tradition. And yet it is seldom the case that a philosophical position can be identified in terms solely of epistemology and logic, or that positions in these areas can exist without corresponding positions on ethics. And in both cases, too great a contrast between personal practical assumptions and philosophical conclusions must cast doubt on the arguments that have produced this result.[5]

Two quotations from Wittgenstein's "A Lecture on Ethics" show the link between the positivist epistemological stance and the professional standing aside from moral involvement which ensued:

> Our words as we use them in science, are vessels capable only of containing and conveying meaning and sense, *natural* meaning and sense. Ethics, if it is anything, is supernatural and our words will only express facts,[6]

and

> The tendency of all men who ever tried to write or talk Ethics or Religion was to run against the boundaries of language. This running against the walls of our cage is perfectly, absolutely hopeless. Ethics

so far as it springs from the desire to say something about the ultimate meaning of life, the absolute good, the absolute valuable, can be no science.[7]

At the same time, the sceptical, or at least agnostic, stance adopted on a wide range of issues in epistemology was accompanied by a corresponding scepticism or agnosticism in ethics. This is not to deny that most of the arguments within this tradition were presented as attempts to refute scepticism—about the existence of material objects, about other minds, about causality, and so on. The overall effect, however, was to divorce commonsense beliefs in these areas from the more sophisticated position of the philosopher. As in the case of the schizophrenia confessed to by Hume, a gap developed between the philosopher in academic discussion and the philosopher in private life who continued to sit on chairs, talk to other people, and make inductive assumptions.

A parallel procedure in ethics results, not surprisingly, in a divorce between the position of the philosopher as an ordinary person participating in the world where "life is made vivid by competing volitions" and the position of the philosopher qua philosopher who, in a professional capacity, has usually sought to avoid, or at least conceal moral commitment.

More recently, it has been a charge of Marxist critics of academic philosophy that there is, nevertheless, a concealed commitment to values even within these, apparently neutral approaches. And, indeed, the values of rationality, impartiality, and equality of respect for individuals are implicit in such discussion—by no means to their detriment. Lack of commitment, then, may be more apparent than real. Nevertheless, a result of the intellectual stance on the part of academic moral philosophy in favour of the avoidance of commitment has been an unwillingness to use the critical tools of philosophy to defend the particular values which, if Marxist critics are right, this type of philosophy actually assumes.

It is also the case that, perhaps by a process of osmosis rather than direct conversion, the crisis of commitment on the part of philosophers has filtered through to the wider community in the form of a widespread position of universal moral toleration, whose logical basis is much more shaky than its extensive adoption justifies. This takes the form of a general aversion to dogmatism on matters of morals, and constitutes a third consequence of the insecurity of evaluation referred to earlier.

The Denial of Dogmatism

To be dogmatic about matters of morals may be to court unpopularity, for it is to be a propagandist for a particular viewpoint that may be vehemently opposed by people of equal but differing conviction. But being a moral dogmatist is not necessarily the same thing as being a moral campaigner. For some form of dogmatism or commitment—a nonstrident attachment to certain moral principles or values—is in fact an essential aspect of morality.

A denial of the need for this sort of dogmatism, though, partly through aversion to the campaigning variety, has become a familiar and widespread attitude. It results from an extension of the notion of tolerance from the sphere of action where it properly belongs, to the sphere of thought and belief where it is essentially incoherent. A comparison with the situation involved in differences of opinion over matters of fact underlines this point. The sense in which I claim to tolerate another person's beliefs about matters of fact that are known by me to be false is quite specific and limited. My toleration consists solely in the fact that I will not actively prevent that person from holding those beliefs. It may or may not extend to refraining from arguing with the person or attempting to alter the beliefs, but it cannot extend to an acceptance or endorsement of the beliefs themselves. For that would be to contradict my own thought and belief.

What is true of factual beliefs is no less true of moral beliefs, convictions, commitments, and valuations. To abstain from proselytizing campaigns is a legitimate and reasonable moral position, though not in all circumstances. Nevertheless, I must be a proselytizer in the sense that I will hold your beliefs, convictions, commitments, and valuations wrong unless they agree with mine. The denial of this type of dogmatism is sometimes equated with liberalism, and liberalism itself then becomes identified with uncritical permissiveness. But these are unnecessary and, for the liberal, damaging conclusions. A liberal position is itself one involving commitment to a particular range of values, and this misunderstanding of what toleration, admittedly one of its prime values, involves is self-destroying.[8]

This position, though rooted in a philosophical mistake, is one of the most pervading popular errors of contemporary culture. The desire to avoid sitting in judgement on one's peers, to desist from moral censure, blame, and opinionated criticism of what is judged to be another's business leads in the end to having no moral business of one's own. For having a defined moral position as far as one's own life is concerned, inevitably, as arguments about universalizability have shown, involves having a defined position about other people's lives as well. While morality is, as was argued earlier, essentially an individual matter, the notion of a purely individual morality in this sense is a contradiction in terms. The only basis on which such a morality could be constructed would be a claim to uniqueness on the part of the individual concerned, and while every individual is indeed unique in morally important ways, differences are dwarfed and overshadowed in matters of valuation by the basic factor of a common humanity.

The Case for Positive Values

These three results of insecurity of evaluation applying respectively to activist groups who adopt a moral but not necessarily philosophical posture, to philosophers who offer meta-ethical but not necessarily moral positions, and to the wider nonphilosophical community, provide a descriptive background to the charge of the essential unfruitfulness of the denial of values. It remains to consider what case can be made out for the positive claim, and here there are two aspects to weigh. First, there is the question of what advantages may accrue from the simple assertion of positive values. And second, since it would be cowardly to retreat, having advanced so far, and since to do so would in effect be to deny the argument that has been advanced already, something must be said about the nature and source of the positive values to be advanced.

The first question is answered to some extent by reversing the argument of the previous sections. Asserting positive values brings a renewal of confidence in the ability of people as independent individual thinkers and agents to reach conclusions on matters of morals, to construct positions and argue for them in the face of opposition or conflicting opinions. This is an essential aspect of respect for reason and for truth. For while it is possible to act collectively, it is not possible to think or reason collectively, whether on matters of morals, on matters of fact, or on matters of logic. Submitting judgement and the construction of ideals to collective arbitration is to sacrifice that respect for reason which must be presumed in anyone prepared to pursue a philosophical argument about the nature of morality any distance at all. So substituting a willingness to assert positive values for the kind of insecurity of evaluation that is signified by a retreat into collective decision making in fact reinstates and reinforces rationality. The reinstatement of reason is something recommended also by Putnam in *Reason, Truth and History*, although he presents this in terms of a defence of ethical objectivity, and a claim that there can be "value facts." He says, for example, "If it can be rational to accept that a picture is beautiful, then it can be a *fact* that the picture is beautiful."[9] Putnam's position could be described as *relative objectivism*, or *objective relativism*—a term that he himself applies to Dewey's ideas. This paradoxical term is no less paradoxical than his own phraseology: "objectivity for us." The notion he proposes is well conveyed in this passage:

> Our conceptions of coherence of acceptability are deeply interwoven with our psychology. They depend upon our biology and our culture; they are by no means "value free." But they *are* our conceptions, and they are conceptions of something real. They define a kind of objectivity, *objectivity for us*, even if it is not the metaphysical objectivity of the God's Eye view. Objectivity and rationality humanly speaking are what we have; they are better than nothing.[10]

Putnam is prepared to make truth fundamentally dependent on value, thus interestingly reversing the usual rejection of values on the ground that truth and falsity do not apply to statements about them.

But no such claim is made here. On the contrary, assigning a place to reason in ethics becomes, according to this view, not solely the prerogative of the ethical objectivist. Nevertheless, the middle ground of Putnam's relative objectivism is the target destination, too, of the notion of positive values as the objects of considered human choice.

This is, though, to return once again to the special position of the philosopher in this debate and to suggest, whether from the viewpoint of a reappraised objectivism, or a reappraised emotivism, a greater willingness to become associated with substantive moral values. Such a willingness must restore a direction for philosophy that outsiders have seen it as lacking since its attempts to jettison ethics met with such a paralysing degree of success. For philosophic commitment has not, after all, left the scene completely. Instead, it has been seen as something to be expected only from Marxists, or from philosphers with a particular religious commitment that provides them with a preformed ethical position. Social concern, in particular, has become identified almost uniquely with the former. Concern for firmness of moral principle, on the other hand, has been preempted by the latter. Within secular but critical traditions of philosophy, relativism or utilitarianism have made the running, the first denigrating principle and the second providing too narrow a focus for social concern.

Finally, a return to unselfconscious dogmatism on the part of the ordinary person is also a return to respect not so much for rationality as for morality itself. Philosophers too readily and too modestly assume a lack of connection between their own ideas and the popular philosophical consciousness. Perhaps, indeed, the idea that there *is* a popular philosophical consciousness will be a novelty to some. But one important area of interest to many people outside philosophy which is nevertheless shaped and influenced by the conclusions of philosophers may be mentioned here as evidence of that connection. This is the area of moral education. R. M. Hare once perceptively remarked that the question of what we should tell our children is the ultimate testing ground of ethical theory.[11] Where moral education is concerned, it has become particularly clear that the ordinary person will detect a route from subjectivist analyses of ethics via uncertainty and insecurity of evaluation to a neutral and uncommitted approach to moral education.[12] Thus one generation's uncertainties unintentionally become the moral nihilism of the next. This result can be countered by restoring the ordinary person's confidence in his or her own moral convictions—or in the justifiability of holding positive values. If many people today have no choice but to cut through the umbilical cord of authoritarian moral justification, it is so much the more important to show that this need not mean the sacrifice of a serious and committed approach to morality. For commitment and radical choice may go hand in hand, and historically and practically it has proved possible to pursue the idea of commitment to common human values—commitment not based on any religious, transcendental, or metaphysical justification—in ways that are free of these kinds of authoritarian links.

For example, the Greek notion of natural law embodied a concept of values which could secure assent simply because they transcended the boundaries of culture and geography—values which were based in the nature of man rather than in any particular social or political arrangements—and even at this early stage, the notion was set against the morally numbing influence of relativism. Again, even then, sceptical attempts were made to link values and moral rules to social hierarchies of power and control, as is illustrated in the conversation with Thrasymachus in Book 1 of Plato's *Republic*. The idea of natural law on its own, though, is too overlaid for the present day with disputable assumptions about human nature and has, moreover, an unacceptably speculative and metaphysical aspect. Its successors today are to be found in the theories of moral development of Piaget and Kohlberg, although this is to turn a notion with an ideal and teleological aspect into something purely naturalistic. Its ideal or aspirational aspect is to be found, however, in the modern notion of human rights which, in spite of uses and abuses, is capable of playing a valuable role on the stage of national and international politics. The idea of human rights, though, is in many ways negative, even if it has positive implications. For this reason it is preferable to augment it, even if it is not possible or desirably wholly to replace it, with the terminology of human values.

This augmentation of the notion allows greater freedom in specifying a substantial moral position. If the aim is to preserve the breadth of appeal across cultures and epochs that notions like natural law and human rights possess, then it is almost bound to be a pluralist conception in which no one value can be dominant. But pluralism does not mean, as MacIntyre suggests, that questions about the good for man are systematically unsettlable. For human interests are varied, and the need to transcend particular localised concerns entails a broad perspective. So the values concerned will include humanity (a concern for human happiness); self-respect (concerned with personal fulfilment); and the traditional liberal values of truth, justice, and freedom. The Kantian principle that people should be treated as ends in themselves and not simply as means or pawns in other people's games will also succinctly sum up many more specific assertions about human rights and freedoms. But since circumstances will inevitably bring occasions when these values must be in conflict with each other, the search for common agreement will always leave scope for individual judgement and appraisal.

There will also be scope for disagreement *about* values, with socialist values, for example, centring on equality and mutual support sometimes being set against liberal values of self-determination and independence. But the ultimate basis of any values, if it is not to be metaphysical, religious, or transcendental can only be choice, so there is no need to make the intuitionist assumption that unanimity of values is inevitable. Recognising this fact reveals the essentially political nature of moral choice. The belief that there cannot be conflict about values generates a moral paralysis that is dissipated by appreciation of the need for alignment between people who have identified and share common values. There is no need, in other words, to adopt the position of universal moral tolerance linked with many forms of relativism. But seeing the need for strength of conviction, and recognising, too, the possibility of being opposed, is not incompatible with the belief that some values have wide human appeal and are more worth pressing than others.

I have chosen the term *positive values* to refer to these values, because the idea of self-chosen values associated with emotivism, subjectivism, and other attitudinal analyses of ethics is the idea of values devoid of content. Self-chosen values, it has been widely assumed in contrasts between ethical subjectivism and objectivism, must be foundationless, impulsive, transitory, immediate, and also particular in their application. At the same time, the corresponding assumption is made that only some metaphysical notion of objective values can import into ethical discussion notions of radical argument, permanency of valuation, and universality of application. The term *positive values* is introduced, therefore, to differentiate these values from the values of the moment with which most forms of ethical subjectivism are associated. Their positive aspect consists in the fact that they represent the objects of a conscious and deliberate search for values that can meet the two conditions as (a) appealing both to people's minds and to their feelings, (i.e., being both intellectually and emotionally satisfying), and (b) doing so in a way that by-passes cultural and social particularities. The effect of the first condition is to entitle us to call them *human* values, and of the second to enable us to talk of *common* human values.

The "common" element in these values is not that something is already "there" to be found, but that each seeker looks for values that he or she can share with others, not as members of the same class or group but simply as other human beings. It is unlikely that values with this kind of intrinsic appeal will be lightly abandoned, or that they will be subjected to frequent change or frequent revision. This is the only sense in which it may be claimed that they are permanent or nontransitory. True, they may be represented as the objects of choice rather than the objects of discovery. Nevertheless, there is an element of discovery in the conception of the quest itself. But because the balance swings marginally in the direction of choice rather than investigation, a search for common human values becomes essentially a political and practical programme rather than a Kantian-style transcendental deduction. The tools to be used in the search for values—even a philosophical search—are negotiation and persuasion rather than logic or intuitive insight. There are, however, investigable psychological and sociological facts, and indeed biological facts, which are relevant to this search, so that it is not solely the province of rhetoric and imagination.

There is nothing arbitrary about reaching conclusions on these values.

That modern moral philosophy must inevitably lead to the conclusion that moral values are arbitrary, ephemeral, and subject to the caprice of the moment was an erroneous understanding of critics who were seeking an essentially authoritarian guarantee of values, such as may be found in religion, law, or tradition. The suggestion here is that it is possible to escape from the choice constantly put before us between, on the one hand, the metaphysical and indefensible represented by the term *objective values*, and, on the other hand, the purely parochial conception of value represented by the claim that values are relative—between the position that moral choice is completely closed and the position that moral choice is completely open.

This is to accept that we have some area of choice where values are concerned, but to deny that the choices involved are fleeting, fluctuating, or arbitrary. We don't, after all, arrive newly at this choice in the present generation, nor is it a matter of purely professional concern for philosophy. It is rather, as J. S. Mill wrote in the last chapter of *Utilitarianism*, that there are "certain classes of moral rules, which concern the essentials of human well-being more nearly, and are therefore of more absolute obligation than any other rules for the guidance of life."[13] In the search for positive values, then, we build on tradition, history, and our cultural inheritance, filtered through our increasing knowledge of the facts of human psychology, physiology, and social tendencies.

The international community has shown itself willing to recognise rules of the kind Mill mentions, and even to legislate their enforcement. It is not to underrate the lapses from these rules that have occurred in practice to say that the notion of violations of human rights, the denial of basic human values, has shown itself to be a powerful political force. As a notion that involves comparing principles with prevailing practices, it has the advantage of being able to be employed not merely by philosophers but by statesmen and politicians and also by groups of individuals working outside the framework of government and politics. The minimal contribution of philosophy must surely be to avoid undermining the theoretical foundations of such intrinsically fruitful and useful notions by confining intelligent choice in ethics to alternatives that ignore it. To have the potential for practical, popular, and widespread appeal is no mean commendation for a notion, and if this can be claimed for the notion of positive values, as opposed to either objective values on the one hand or purely relative values on the other, then the onus is on those who would oppose it to justify their position.

Notes

This paper, in its original form, was presented as part of a symposium to the Joint Session of the Mind Association and the Aristotelian Society that took place in Bangor, North Wales, in July 1983. The paper, together with a reply by Andrew Collier, was published in the *Proceedings of the Aristotelian Society*, supp. vol. 57 (1983): 17–35, and is reprinted here by permission of the editor and publishers.

1. A. MacIntyre, *After Virtue* (London: Duckworth, 1981), p. 25.
2. H. Reichenbach, *The Rise of Scientific Philosophy* (Berkeley: University of California Press, 1951), p. 297.
3. A. J. Ayer, "On the Analysis of Moral Judgements," in *Philosophical Essays* (London: Macmillan, 1954), p. 242.
4. MacIntyre, *After Virtue*, p. 209. See also chap. 3, pp. 22–34.
5. For a more extended discussion of the contribution made by the moral philosophy of G. E. Moore and A. J. Ayer, see chap. 8.
6. L. Wittgenstein, "A Lecture on Ethics," *Philosophical Review* 74 (1965): 7.
7. Ibid., pp. 11–12.
8. For fuller argument on this point, see chap. 10, pp. 125–134.
9. H. Putnam, *Reason, Truth and History* (Cambridge: Cambridge University Press, 1981), p. x.
10. Ibid., p. 55.
11. R. M. Hare, "Principles," *Proceedings of the Aristotelian Society* 73 (1972–3): pp. 1–18.
12. For an argument to show that this is not a necessary sequence of connections, see chap. 6, pp. 69–76.
13. J. S. Mill, *Utilitarianism* (1859: reprint, London: Dent, 1954), p. 55.

Index of Names

Archambault, R. D. 57, 67, 76
Arendt, H. 53, 56
Aristotle, 92
Atkinson, R. F. 71, 76
Austin, J. L. 57, 91
Ayer, A. J. 4, 12, 91, 101–111, 112, 137, 150

Bambrough, R. 111
Bayle, P. 50, 56
Bell, C. 162
Bell, D. 6, 12
Berkeley, G. 19, 24
Berlin, I. 128, 134
Bradley, F. 6, 7, 12, 94
Broad, C. D. 106, 112
Brooke, R. 94

Callicot, J. B. 20–21, 24
Carnap, R. 102, 104, 106
Carson, R. 15, 24
Club of Rome, 16
Cohen, M. R. 20, 24
Collier, A. 150
Cornford, F. M. 56

Devlin, P. 29, 41, 131, 134
Dewey, J. 59, 79, 145

Ewing, A. C. 93

Feigl, H. 102, 112
Flew, A. 62
Foot, P. 4, 12, 63, 67
Frankena, W. K. 111

Gellner, E. A. 118, 123
Gödel, K. 102
Godwin, W. 39, 41
Goodin, R. 20, 24
Gregory XVI, Pope, 51

Haack, R. 61, 67
Hägerström, A. 106, 112
Harding, W. H. 20, 24
Hare, R. M. 111, 119, 146, 150
Hargreaves, D. 78, 80, 89
Harrington, J. 51, 56
Hart, H. L. A. 131, 134
Hayek, F. 11
Heisenberg, W. 22, 24–25
Hempel, C. G. 112
Hirsch, F. 17, 24
Hobhouse, L. T. 55, 56
Hollins, T. H. B. 76
Hospers, J. 111
Hudson, W. D. 12
Hume, D. 3–4, 12, 62, 63, 102–103, 104, 112, 142

Iltis, H. H. 17, 24

Kamen, H. 56
Kant, I. 92, 103, 114, 139
Keynes, J. M. 94, 111
King, P. 54, 55, 56
Klemke, E. D. 111
Kohlberg, L. 147
Kuhn, T. 50

Langford, G. 59, 67
Laslett, P. 56
Leopold, A. 14, 17, 21, 24
Levy, P. 111
Locke, D. 41
Luther, M. 50

MacIntyre, A. 63, 67, 117–121, 123, 135, 138, 139, 147, 150
Malcolm, N. 111
Mannison, D. 24
Marcuse, H. 45, 46, 51, 52, 55, 56, 79
Marx, K. 11, 110, 136
Midgley, M. 18, 24, 63, 67

Mill, J. S. 47, 48, 49, 51, 52, 56, 149, 150
Milton, J. 50
Moore, B. 55
Moore, G. E. 57, 91–101, 102, 103, 104, 105, 111, 112, 150
Murdy, W. H. 24

McCloskey, H. J. 15, 24, 25
McRobbie, M. 24

Neurath, O. 102

O'Connor, D. J. 59, 67
Ogden, C. K. 105
O'Hear, A. 12
Orwell, G. 38, 51

Partington, G. 80, 89
Passmore, J. 18, 24, 112
Pateman, T. 79, 89
Paul, G. A. 111
Pericles, 52
Peters, R. S. 57, 59, 61, 67, 74, 81
Piaget, J. 147
Plato, 30, 52, 56, 58, 79, 92, 146
Popper, K. 11, 22, 24, 50
Prichard, H. 93
Putnam, H. 53, 145, 150

Rand, A. 15, 24
Reichenbach, H. 136, 150
Rhees, R. 1, 12
Richards, I. A. 105, 112
Ross, W. D. 93
Routley, R. 21, 24
Routley, V. 21, 24
Runciman, W. G. 56
Russell, B. 27, 38, 41, 70, 76, 93–94, 111
Ryle, G. 59, 67

Salisbury Review, 6, 12
Santayana, G. 39–40, 41
Sartre, J. P. 110, 121–122
Scherer, D. and Attig, T. 24
Schilpp, P. A. 111, 112
Schlick, M. 102, 104, 106, 112
Searle, J. 4, 12, 63, 67
Sellars, W. 111, 112
Shelley, P. B. 27, 41
Society for Applied Philosophy, 6, 12, 110
Socinus, F. 50
Stevenson, C. L. 112
Stone, C. D. 24
Strachey, L. 94, 111
Sugarman, B. 76

Talmon, J. 11
Tredwell, R. 111
Trotsky, L. 61, 67

Urban, G. R. and Glenny, M. 24
Urmson, J. O. 112

Vienna Circle, 57, 102

Waismann, F. 102, 112
Wall, G. 71, 74, 76
Ward, B. and Dubos, R. 24
Wardle, R. M. 41
Warnock, G. 100, 111
Weinreich-Haste, H. 25
Williams, N. 76
Wilson, J. 71, 76
Wisdom, J. 57
Wittgenstein, L. 1, 12, 102, 103, 112, 141–142, 150
Wolfenden Report, 131
Wolff, R. P. 52, 53, 55
Wollstonecraft, M. 41
Woolf, L. 94
Woolf, V. 94